NONCOMMISSIONED
TRUTH
OF
9-11-2001

Noncommissioned Truth of 9-11-2001
Copyright © 2015 Tomas Pimentel

All rights reserved. No part of this book may be reproduced (except for inclusion in reviews), disseminated or utilized in any form or by any means, electronic or mechanical, including photocopying, recording, or in any information storage and retrieval system, or the Internet/World Wide Web without written permission from the author or publisher.

Noncommissioned Truth of 9-11-2001
Tomas Pimentel

1. Title   2. Author   3. Politics & Social Sciences

Library of Congress Control Number: 2014920915
ISBN 13: 978-0-692-33552-9

NONCOMMISSIONED
TRUTH
OF
9-11-2001

Tomas Pimentel

*To Thomas Pimentel Jr., who assumed the watch of the sentry
to guard the Constitution of this great nation,
the United States of America.*

*To my wife, Miriam Pimentel, and my kids,
Tamara, Jeannie, Magnie, and Victor,
who supported me during my service in the US Navy.*

Acknowledgments

So many people have helped in the creation of this book that it would be impossible to name each one. But every little thing that was contributed was of great importance, from photos to details of missions and dates. IBU-24, I will always be grateful for a team that was there for each other. The camaraderie and friendship that were born of this team will be bonded forever. We still look after one another long after those missions. Thank you, IBU-24, for allowing me to be a part of the brotherhood that still exists today.

Introduction

The terrorist attacks perpetrated against the United States of America on September 11, 2001, took our nation by surprise. This is a fact. We did not expect a group of militant religious and cultural extremists to hijack our own planes in our own airspace and use them as fully loaded missiles with which to demolish our buildings, our people, our sense of hope, and our way of life. But that was exactly what they did. Aside from the thousands of human lives snuffed out so violently and horrifyingly, and the destruction of renowned architecture and real estate over three states, these terrorists succeeded in changing how we lived. On that day, in a matter of hours, we became fearful and distrustful of the world around us and even, sometimes, of one another. We became violent too, as this tragedy drove us to seek revenge on those we thought were responsible. Unfortunately, the blame we've laid has sometimes been erroneous. In our zealousness to make sense of what happened, we lashed out at people and groups who had nothing to do with it.

This is the point of terrorism: to make us so scared we can no longer go on with our lives as they were before, show us how vulnerable we are, and plant seeds of doubt in our minds about who we can trust and what our government is or isn't doing to protect us. At least that's the simple definition, one that is easy for laypeople to digest. But on a higher level, the subject of terrorism is difficult and complex—so much so that the global community cannot even agree on one legally binding definition. Most will concede it involves factors such as the following:

- Violent acts meant to instill fear in or intimidate a population.
- Religious motives, political motives, or sometimes both.
- Civilian targets.
- Widespread psychological trauma.

However, these points are quite vague whereas terrorism is most certainly not: It is anything but black and white. One person might see a terrorist as a religious extremist while another would consider him a freedom fighter sacrificing himself for a just cause. It's all in the interpretation and the worldview with which one approaches it. After all, even Nelson Mandela—recipient of the Nobel Peace Prize in 1993—was put on the US terrorism watch list under the Reagan administration, and he remained on it until as recently as 2008.

If there is one overarching statement we can pull from all acts of terrorism, it is a desire for publicity. Such attacks are steeped in symbolism and, in fact, often go after iconic targets—such as the World Trade Center and the Pentagon. These two were hubs of US business and the US military, respectively, two areas that terrorists generally wish to undermine, as crippling our finance and defense systems could leave us vulnerable on many fronts. Often they seek to demolish such institutions or locales specifically because doing so will garner maximal media coverage, which is an essential goal of terrorism. The more press they get, the more fear they instill, thus compelling the government of the nation under siege to either undertake a particular action or stop one that is already underway in order to quell the population's fears and, hopefully, ward off further attacks.

However, that tactic has *never* worked against the United States. We are never intimidated, and we do not back down, not even in the face of violence. Once we were over the shock of what had happened on that fateful autumn day in 2001, we rallied ourselves, as we always do. We Americans are a strong people. We rise above; we overcome. And out of the ashes of the World Trade Center, the Pentagon, and a barren field in Shanksville, Pennsylvania, arose a new sense of determination and hope. We banded together against our common foe—those who seek to destroy the very fabric of our great nation—and sent out a very clear message: We will not be defeated. We will mourn, yes. We will never forgive, and we certainly will not forget. But we will rebuild, and we will continue on. And, of course, we will be better than ever.

This is the American way.

Still, some people wanted answers. In fact, they still do. The purpose of the 9/11 attacks was clear: to undermine the safety and security of our citizens and foment distrust in our leaders by showing that they—supposedly—could not protect us from harm. Yet many people do not accept that at face value. They are sure there is some underlying meaning, some person or people or entity at whom we can point our fingers, someone other than the actual terrorists who committed the crimes or at least were complicit in them, whether actively or passively. I have never understood this point of view or these conspiracy theories. What do they solve? How do they help the situation? All they do is add to the confusion and fear that terrorism creates. They fan the flames of an already blazing topic. So I tend to discount what people who believe them have to say.

Then there are others who know that 9/11 was real, and that it happened for a very specific reason: A group of men made a plan to get on some airplanes, hijack them, and fly them into populated buildings and areas in our country. Then they carried out that plan. But this group of skeptics also believes that 9/11 happened due to the fact that—to use an often-quoted phrase—America was sleeping. We were not watching our ports; our government agencies were either not listening to or not heeding the "chatter," as they call it, or the communications between terrorist groups and operatives around the world. These people do not exactly blame the United States for what happened to us, but they do not release it from responsibility either. The government could have, and should have, done more to prevent such a tragedy from occurring.

I do not fall into this camp, either. In fact I believe exactly the opposite. No, I *know* the opposite is true. As a member of the US Navy (now retired), I saw firsthand the many measures our military and our government have undertaken to safeguard our citizens and our way of life. Not only that, but I have helped make it all happen. In my military career I protected the waters of the Atlantic Ocean off the East Coast of the United States, on constant watch for any vessels entering our waters or other possible threats. I also patrolled the New York Harbor during times when terrorist attacks could have been imminent—when the government *was* listening to the chatter and taking it very seriously, just as it always has done and always will do. Fortunately, either those plans never came to fruition or we thwarted them before they became serious, and the public never knew anything had happened at all.

I am not here to give away those secrets. This book is not a tell-all about the failings or triumphs of the American government, especially in the war on terrorism. If you want commentary on that, just turn to the Internet—there are an endless number of websites presenting both positive and negative views on this subject. You're bound to find something with which you agree. And whatever your opinion, I would not refute it. You are entitled to your beliefs, just like every other American—including me. And this is my view: We are ready. We have always been ready. We were not and are not sleeping. It's just that sometimes things happen that are beyond our human control. Things we cannot foresee simply because they have never happened before—like two passenger jets, full of people and fuel, flying into the World Trade Center on a beautiful, sunny Tuesday morning.

I am not here to debate facts or to rehash the events of that fateful morning. These you can and probably have read about in any number of newspapers and magazines and on websites, not to mention the myriad TV shows and even feature movies that have been produced covering the events of 9/11 from just about every angle. Instead, in these pages I will present a case for the vigilance of the US military and federal government and explain, through my firsthand knowledge and experience, how we have dealt with terrorism historically and through the present day. My aim is to show that we have never once fallen asleep at the wheel, particularly not on September 11. We have protected and served the people of this great nation to the best of our ability and then some; it is in our nature to always go above and beyond the call of duty.

I hope that you will find what I have to say here not only informative but enlightening and inspiring. I hope it brings you a sense of security if you need one, or reassurance that there are forces looking out for you even if you are not aware of them. Most of all, I hope it proves to you that America is in fact wide awake.

One

It is without question that the US armed forces, particularly the navy, are without equal in the world today. We are still the world's most powerful and effective fleet, with more than 1.3 million active military personnel across the army, navy, air force, and marines. In this respect we are second in the world only to China, but, to be fair, they have a population of 1.35 billion while ours is only 313 million. The United States also has 850,880 reserve military personnel, or individuals who are not full-time soldiers but are on call and ready to be mobilized whenever they are needed.

Given all this, there is no doubt that we can prevail over almost any adversary in almost any situation, especially when our many political and military allies around the world are able and willing to offer their support. This includes all NATO nations and their territories by extension; independent countries such as Tonga, Jamaica, Belize, Samoa, Palau, and Micronesia; countries with which we have mutual defense agreements, such as Japan and Korea; non-NATO European countries including Ireland, Sweden, and Malta; and *sui generis* nations (meaning their governments are unique or unusual, or somehow do not fit into standard governmental molds) such as Afghanistan and Honduras. In total we can count on 104 of the world's countries and territories to have our back when it's against the wall—or when we're out there helping other people to fight for their freedom and independence.

This might sound like hyperbole or jingoist rhetoric, but it is simply the truth. Since the end of World War II, the United States has held a position of absolute naval supremacy, even as rivals such as the former Soviet Union developed their own admittedly strong and substantial military operations during the Cold War, a period of political and military tensions between the United States and our NATO allies and the Soviet Union (or the USSR) and its allies. The Cold War stretched across decades—roughly from 1946 to 1991—and though there were no major wars between the two sides, both played opposing supporting roles in many smaller-scale battles; for example, in Korea, Vietnam, and Afghanistan. We both also armed ourselves to an extreme degree in preparation for the next world war, which was always an underlying threat. Of course these weapons were nuclear, assuring mutually assured destruction should either faction choose to employ them. This meant that if the Soviets launched a nuclear attack on us, we had a plan in place to launch our own missiles and wipe them off the map. Thus both nations would be destroyed at the same time—mutual destruction. And you can bet the USSR had the same provisions in place for us.

It was during this era that the term *superpower* became a part of our common vocabulary; though the word itself had existed since 1920, during the Cold War we heard it every day on the news and in other media to describe both the United States and the USSR. Over the many years of this war, we fought with one another over our profound ideological, political, and economic differences. The Soviet Union, for example, was a communist society. This means its leadership believed in common ownership of production capital such as machinery, tools, and factories but did not believe in upholding the order of social classes or using money. As totalitarians as well, they also believed the state held complete authority over all of society and rightfully could control all public and even private matters of its people.

The United States, on the other hand, was and still is (at least in theory) a liberal democracy. This means we elect our leaders via fair and free elections, we separate the government's power into different branches (in our case the legislative, meaning Congress and the Senate; judicial, or the Supreme Court; and executive, which refers solely to the president), we have a constitution as a political and social contract, and we seek to protect the rights of individuals through the laws we create.

Sometimes our two countries were civil to one another, as in the 1970s, when we entered a period of *détente*, or an easing of the strained relations. We even broached the subject of limiting nuclear arms. But then there were the 1980s. The Soviets entered the decade entrenched in a war with Afghanistan, a nation that had thus far remained neutral in the Cold War. In September 1983 a Soviet pilot shot down a Korean passenger plane flying through Soviet airspace, killing all 269 crew and passengers aboard, including sitting congressman Lawrence McDonald of Georgia. Three months later the Soviets mistook some NATO military exercises and simulations as the real thing and believed the United States and its allies were preparing to launch a nuclear attack. Needless to say, whatever positive relations we'd been building fell by the wayside before the decade even reached its halfway point.

I joined the navy toward the end of that era, in 1987. I was living in the Bronx, New York, at the time; I was twenty-seven years old and had emigrated from the Dominican Republic to the United States about seven years earlier. I was also unemployed in 1987, and the military seemed like a good career option. So I enlisted.

At that time the work of the US Navy was, as were all military branches, focused largely on the Soviet Union and followed these three main objectives:

1. To deter and prevent the possibility of nuclear war.
2. To defend the United States and our allies against Soviet aggression.
3. To protect US interests around the world from smaller-scale Soviet aggression, specifically in developing nations.

But our focus was soon to change. In the same year that I enrolled to serve, trouble was brewing in the Middle East. The ongoing conflict in the region was like a snowball rolling downhill, gathering momentum and size as it went. Iraq turned its attention to Kuwait, a neighboring country, and we increased our military operations in response. We sent warships to escort and protect both Kuwaiti and US oil tankers as they navigated the Persian Gulf.

Then, on May 17, 1987, the Iraqi Air Force attacked and damaged the USS *Stark* in the Persian Gulf, killing thirty-seven navy personnel. The United States had been keeping a military presence in the region due to the Iran-Iraq War, which was in full swing at the time. Also known as the First Persian Gulf

War, this conflict had begun in 1980, when Iraq had invaded Iran following a long history of border disputes, or confrontations over possession and control of certain parcels of land. At the time, Iran was also undergoing an internal revolution, led by the Ayatollah Khomeini, in which the government had been overthrown and replaced by an Islamic republic; Iraq feared this would cause an uprising of the Shia majority in its own country as well and so took advantage of the chaos of the moment and attacked Iran without warning. Iran quickly beat them back and regained all the land they had lost but remained on the offensive for years. The conflicts continued into the late 1980s.

On April 14, 1988, another US ship, the guided-missile frigate USS *Samuel B. Roberts* struck a mine set in the Persian Gulf by the Iranian forces; the explosion created a twenty-five-foot hole in the ship's hull, but it did not sink, and no lives were lost. After this incident, US Navy divers discovered there were other Iranian mines in the area.

On April 18, 1988, we launched a retaliation known as Operation Praying Mantis, in which we attacked three Iranian oil platforms with two groups of surface action groups, or SAGs. The first, which was directed to the Sassan oil platform, consisted of the destroyers USS *Merrill* and USS *Lynde McCormick*, and aircraft from the carriers USS *Enterprise* and USS *Truxtun*. We also utilized the USS *Trenton*, an amphibious transport dock, and the helicopter detachment from the USS *Samuel B. Roberts*. At 8:00 a.m., we sent a radio warning to the Sassan platform, advising its occupants to abandon it. Twenty minutes later, our helicopters opened fire until the platform's ZU-23 guns were disabled, ceasing only once upon request so a transport of personnel could depart from the rig. Then the marines moved in for reconnaissance. They recovered some small arms and some classified intelligence.

Next, the unit was ordered to do the same to the Rahksh oil platform, which was north of their current location. En route they were attacked by two Iranian F-4s, which our *Lynde McCormick* headed off by locking the jets in its fire-control radar, indicating it would retaliate. At that point the command called the SAG back and canceled the Rahksh attack so as to de-escalate the situation with the Iranians.

The second SAG included the USS *Wainwright*, a guided-missile cruiser, and two frigates—the USS *Simpson* and the USS *Bagley*. These were assigned to attack the Sirri oil platform; as part of the operation, Navy SEALs would then occupy and destroy the rig. However, when they got there they saw the platform had already been severely damaged by previous naval gunfire, and the assault was called off.

The action escalated. The Iranians sent out speedboats to attack targets in the Persian Gulf, including vessels belonging to the United States, Panama, and England. The USS *Simpson*, USS *Wainwright*, and USS *Bagley* were involved in a skirmish with an attacking Iranian Combattante II Kaman-class fast-attack craft, in which the latter was ultimately crippled. Iran sent out F-4 Phantom fighters and frigates armed with surface-to-air missiles and fired Silkworm missiles from land in attempts to take out our units.

Finally, the US defense secretary ordered the navy to stand down—to give Iran a way out, as our forces were clearly obliterating theirs. Iran accepted; both sides remained guarded, but the hostilities ceased.

Over the next three years, the US military fought battles and defended freedom in Honduras, Panama, Libya, Columbia, Bolivia, Peru, the Philippines, and Liberia. Then, in 1990, we went back to the Middle East. The friendly relations Iraq and Kuwait had managed to build after the Iran-Iraq War had begun to erode due to a myriad of diplomatic and economic factors. The growing tensions culminated in Iraq invading Kuwait in August of that year. Within two days, most of the Kuwaiti military was defeated or had fled to neighboring nations. Saddam Hussein, the despot Iraqi leader, declared his victory and annexed Kuwait as a province of Iraq, then set his sights on Saudi Arabia. If he could have overtaken that nation too, he would have had control of the majority of the world's oil reserves (along with his own in Iraq and what he'd claimed in Kuwait).

King Fahd, the leader of Saudi Arabia, had already called on the United States for military help by that point, and now he renewed the request. In less than a week, President George H. W. Bush, acting under the Carter Doctrine (established by President Jimmy Carter in 1980, stating the United States will use military force if necessary to defend its interests in the Persian Gulf), launched Operation Desert Shield and deployed our armed forces once again to the Gulf region. Thirty-four other nations did the same—countries as far-reaching as Argentina, Norway, the Philippines, and Senegal along with larger world powers, such as France, the United Kingdom, Spain, and so on. In addition, Germany and Japan provided financial support. This turned out to be the largest coalition of nations since World War II. But the majority of the coalition's forces came from the United States, and I was among the soldiers who answered that call. I served aboard the USS *Nitro*, an ammunition ship carrying supplies for the USS *Wisconsin*. Specifically, I was an electrician aboard the *Nitro*.

The defense of Saudi Arabia lasted until January 1991, at which time the operation was shifted to become Operation Desert Storm, an air-land battle in which we brought the fight directly to Hussein in Iraq. On January 17, we launched an aerial attack to drive the Iraqi army at last out of Kuwait and followed it up with a ground assault on February 24. Our mission was successful; the Iraqi troops receded, and the Coalition forces advanced. The entire ground conflict lasted for only one hundred hours.

Afterward some criticized President Bush for not capturing Baghdad, the capital of Iraq, and overthrowing Hussein's regime. Whether or not that would have been a good move at the time is a debatable point, but such a move definitely would have had high political and human costs that we just did not want to risk. President Bush officially declared a cease fire on February 28. The United Nations passed a resolution of the cease-fire terms the following April.

Looking back, some people view our operations in and around Iraq as the seeds that eventually grew into today's war on terrorism. And this is not outside the realm of possibility. After all, we'd put Iraq on our list of state sponsors of terrorism in 1979 due to their support of militant groups like the Palestinian Abu Nidal Organization. But then we removed them from the list in 1982 in order to assist them during the Iran-Iraq War—or, more accurately, to prevent an Iranian victory. From that point on, even though the US government was well aware that Iraq had continued ties to and involvement in terrorism, we forged strategic bonds with Saddam Hussein. Sometimes, as they say, we must keep our friends close and our enemies closer.

What really drove the terrorism behind the September 11 attacks, however, had little to do with Iraq. After Operation Desert Storm, and particularly after the subsequent Second Gulf War in 2003, the United States maintained a presence in Saudi Arabia—which, according to some, violated the Muslim prophet Muhammad's edict against a "permanent presence of infidels in Arabia." Among those believers was Osama bin Laden, who we now know was the mastermind behind the September 11 terrorist attacks. Some critics called our military presence there an occupation; some activists criticized it as tacit support of the House of Saud, the nation's ruling family, who have been referred to as totalitarians and dictators. But the fact remained that we maintained our troops in Saudi Arabia because the government had asked us to be there and continued to allow us to remain there. We withdrew only in 2003, when US Secretary of Defense Donald Rumsfeld declared that year's Iraq War no longer needed our support, and he brought the majority of our forces stationed there home.

Two

I served as a full-time soldier in the US Navy for four years. In July 1991, I returned from serving in Iraq, and shortly after that, in September, my tour of duty ended. But I did stay on in the Navy Reserve, doing the same sort of electrical engineering work that I had done while I was deployed. Members of the reserve are required to attend three days of training, or drilling, per month, usually a Friday, Saturday, and Sunday. I was sent to Cape May, New Jersey, to be part of a team of minesweepers patrolling off the East Coast of the United States. We worked out of the Coast Guard Training Center Cape May—the fifth-largest base in the Coast Guard and the only one at which newly enlisted personnel, all of which are civilian volunteers, are trained for duty.

Our craft, the *Coopminer*, was an eighty-four-foot wooden ship equipped with a sonar system. Sonar, a loose acronym for sound navigation and ranging, uses sound propagation to detect objects underwater. We would drop hydrophones, or microphones specially developed to listen to and record sounds underwater, and track all detectable movements in the ocean. Since this was during peacetime, much of our work was training to be ready for situations of aggression, should they occur. For example, we practiced listening for submarines that might come near the coast. If an enemy or unidentified submarine came into our waters or was trying to do so in stealth, the sonar could pick up the sounds of the sub's movement through the water as well as its engine noises and other ambient audio.

The sonar could also tell us the vessel's country of origin, what it was used for in that country, and its name. Once we had this information, we would follow whatever course of procedure was called for in that instance; for example, initiating contact with the captain of the vessel to ask for identification and authorization to be in US waters or tracking the sub with no contact to see if it left our domain on its own. During my time on this mission, we did discover vessels in this way from time to time, though I am not at liberty to disclose when or where, or from what country they originated. Just please rest easy in knowing that our military maintains a vigilant watch on our coasts. If a potential threat comes in, we will meet it first and deal with it appropriately.

On the *Coopminer* we also swept the ocean floor using sonar technology, looking for lost objects or items that did not belong there. This meant we did not have to send a diver down into the water, thus eliminating the risks that entailed, including any number of issues with the diving equipment or contact with any objects that might be weaponized or otherwise dangerous. We did find things every so often, though mostly just debris from boats that had passed through or trash from the shore that had drifted out to sea and sunk. We also searched areas for what might pose threats to naval operations; for instance, mines or any other explosive devices that could have been planted at the bottom of the ocean for later detonation. Fortunately, we found none of these during my watch.

I was still stationed in Cape May in 1993, when a group of

terrorists from the radical Muslim extremist group al-Qaeda detonated a truck bomb in a parking garage underneath the North Tower of the World Trade Center in New York. Six people were killed, and many were injured not just physically but emotionally as well. The terrorists' aim had been to cause the North Tower to topple over onto the South Tower, thus taking both of them down. It did not work, but they did succeed in creating fear and anxiety in the people of New York and indeed the rest of the nation—one of the aims and the true definition of *terrorism*.

Nowadays, everyone knows who al-Qaeda is; since the terrorist attacks of September 11, 2001, the name of the group and its founder and leader, Osama bin Laden, have become household words, flashing across TV screens and newspaper headlines even now, more than a decade after the fact. But back in 1993, the organization was practically unheard of by the general public. It originated in the Soviet war in Afghanistan as a collection of *mujahideen* (Muslims who engage in *jihad*, or the inner spiritual and/or outer physical struggle to fulfill one's duties to Allah; today the Western world largely associates the term with terrorism and radical, militant Islam) fighters against the Soviet-backed Afghan government. Because this was in the midst of one of the worst decades of the Cold War, the United States supported this opposition to the Soviet communist attempt to take over the nation, which President Carter had called "the greatest threat to peace since the Second World War." Both Carter and his successor, President Reagan, approved of funding for this and other anti-communist and guerilla resistance groups through the CIA's Operation Cyclone program.

So where did al-Qaeda's apparent animosity toward the United States come from? When the Soviet Union withdrew from Afghanistan in 1989, bin Laden returned to his native Saudi Arabia and offered his group's services to King Fahd, to bolster the outnumbered Saudi army against the Iraqi invaders. But the king declined, preferring instead to seek military assistance from the United States.

This snub angered bin Laden, who considered this foreign presence in his faith's most holy land a violation, as mentioned earlier, of Muhammad's prohibition of infidel installations in Saudi Arabia. It was profane and blasphemous, the worst kind of insult the West in general and the United States in particular could have perpetrated against his religion. Bin Laden was so avid in this belief, he made his feelings known publicly to the House of Saud—and was promptly exiled from his beloved homeland. Needless to say, his anger and resentment only grew from that point on, but we will examine that further later on in this book.

When the FBI's investigation into the 1993 World Trade Center bombing revealed that al-Qaeda was behind it, we realized we were facing a new enemy, one with a "one soldier, one mission" mentality, similar to the Japanese kamikazes of World War II. Their sole purpose was to fly their planes into Navy ships; that was all they were trained for. The only difference between them and the terrorists of al-Qaeda was that the Japanese wore uniforms and had specific targets, showing discipline in their military planning and execution. These new terrorists were and continue to be indiscriminate. They choose targets without consideration of who they will be killing—men, women, and children; we are all the same to them. Their only concern is killing and inflicting as much damage as possible on the people of the United States. They want us to be afraid.

This was a shocking revelation and an eye opener. On the heels of this discovery came the further realization that the United States did not have a fighting force to combat this new sort of enemy, but our government and military set out to form one immediately on all fronts. Toward this end, in 1994 the navy converted the minesweeping team I was on into a force-protection and antiterrorism unit called Inshore Boat Unit 24 (IBU-24). We were chosen for this team specifically because of our commitment to serving our country and each other, the members of our unit. This level of dedication was necessary because each person on IBU-24 had to be ready to deploy within twenty-four hours of notification if necessary. The navy even sent people to our jobs and our homes at random times to make sure they knew where we were in case of emergency. And because the IBU-24 was classified as a priority-1 unit, we often drilled for more than the three days per month that the reserve mandated.

Obviously, this assignment required full commitment to the mission and an ability to put service before one's personal life. Understandably, not everyone who was appointed to the team would last because of the hardships this unpredictable schedule could create.

As I mentioned, one of the duties of the IBU-24 was force protection, which means we helped to safeguard other navy units as they carried out their orders, particularly in dangerous locales or high-threat situations. The specific purpose of this unit at the time was to guard the city of New York, which, as one of the world's most populated cities and a hub of world finance, has always been a salient target for terrorists. Prior to my team's assignment there, another unit—the IBU-23—had done the same job, patrolling and guarding the waters and shores of New York—but that team was dismantled in 1995 under recommendations from the Defense Base Closure and Realignment Commission, an independent board of defense-policy experts convened by Congress in 1988, during the Reagan administration, to decide which military bases in the United States could be closed down due to the reduction in the size of our military forces after the end of the Cold War. The commission made such recommendations in 1988, 1991, and 1993, all of which were adopted by Congress and the president.

In 1995, the commission again submitted a package of proposed cuts, including the closure of twenty-eight major military bases, the realignment of twenty-two major bases, and the closure or realignment of many minor bases. On July 13 of that year, President Clinton accepted the recommendations, and in the process of executing the orders it entailed, the IBU-23 was effectively taken out of service.

In 1996, my unit, the IBU-24, was assembled to pick up that team's main mission of guarding New York City. At the time, our unit was based out of Fort Dix, located about sixteen miles south of Trenton, the capital of New Jersey. Historically, Fort Dix had been a US army training base; new recruits had been inducted into the armed forces via basic training there since 1917. In the late 1980s, under recommendations from the aforementioned Defense Base Closure and Realignment Commission, the base was to be closed, but advocates and interested parties were able to keep it open as an army reserve training center, which it still operates as today. Up to fifteen thousand military personnel report to Fort Dix for training each weekend, and since the September 11, 2001, terrorist attacks, it has served as a major mobilization point for both the reserves and the National Guard.

Later, in 2009, Fort Dix merged with a US Air Force facility and a US Navy facility to become the Joint Base McGuire-Dix-Lakehurst (JB MDL). Though even today it is still commonly known as just Fort Dix, it is now a FORSCOM power projection platform for the northeastern United States.

At the time when the IBU-24 was assembled in the summer of 1994, though, Fort Dix was still under the command of the army reserves, with air force and navy facilities close by. This meant that by basing our unit out of Fort Dix, we would have easy, fast access to C5 (inflatable) boats, jets, or whatever we needed for our antiterrorism missions. We had six twenty-seven-foot aluminum-hull patrol boats of our own as well, powered by twin inboard/outboard diesel engines, and each could be equipped with .50-caliber machine guns, M60 machine guns, MK-19 grenade launchers, and other small arms as necessary.

As soon as the IBU-24 was created, my team and I were assigned to a boat. We started training immediately, to learn as much as we could to get us to the level of being deployable; we went from base to base, learning different military tactics from each of the armed forces. In April 1995, we spent two weeks back in Cape May, to participate in Allegiant Sentry 95, a major exercise held at the Coast Guard's Recruit Training Center. During this time, we trained with members of the Delta Force (the 1st Special Forces Operational Detachment-Delta, one of the United States's primary antiterrorism units) and the Navy

SEALs (Sea, Air, and Land Teams; the navy's principal special-operations force) to learn all aspects of land warfare. Members of the Coast Guard taught us small-boat navigational safety, lighting systems, how to recognize the risks and dangers of small boats, and navigational tactics when operating in rough waters, such as how to ride high waves to keep the boat from capsizing. Navigating small boats is not as easy as it may seem, especially when riding a wave that's fifteen or even thirty feet high. Such circumstances often result in injuries, from torn tendons and muscles to broken limbs.

We also drilled with port security and the Marine Corps on the Coast Guard training camp's open exercise field. At one point, there were a couple days of very heavy rain and the field became saturated and muddy, which was almost worse than the rain itself. With 500 military personnel marching over and across it all day and often into the night, plus numerous trucks and Humvees driving back and forth, it became a big mess very quickly. On top of that, we were all sleeping in tents that leaked so badly, we might as well have slept out on the open field in the rain. It was complete chaos at times, but it was also a good and valuable lesson: As soldiers, we had to learn to deal with whatever Mother Nature could throw at us.

No matter what the weather, however—and it did clear up after those couple of days—each day at Allegiant Sentry would start the same. After breakfast, at about 7:30 a.m., the commanding officer (CO) would read the POD—the plan of the day—that he and all other department heads had collectively constructed the previous evening. This was basically a list of all the things that needed to be done in a day and to ensure that all personnel were employed in productive ways. During the

Tent city during Allegiant Sentry/first antiterrorism training.

POD call we would also have roll call and personnel inspections, in which the CO would inspect our appearances to verify that we were displaying military standard dress and grooming.

When the CO dismissed us, we reported for whatever duty we were to complete that day—say, to drill at sea with the Port Security Unit (PSU) 305, a Coast Guard unit providing counterterrorism support to domestic ports in the United States. (If the navy needs them, however, they can go to other countries.) We would board the designated boat and head out to complete whatever specific tasks had been outline for us in the POD, such as dropping off personnel for missions or picking them up after missions were completed. We also learned the protocols for transporting high-value assets, or HVA, such as artillery or ammunition, the loss of which could seriously negatively impact the United States' military (particularly war-fighting) capabilities or in some way be of benefit to an enemy.

During this intensive training, we also received instruction in defense for all types of warfare and any battle scenarios that might arise. In the days of old, soldiers were taught how to shoot their guns and shimmy under enemy lines. In the modern world, those lines are not always clear, and the type of war we were facing then—and still face today—was unlike anything we'd ever seen. Our enemies used to wear uniforms that identified their ranks and where they were from, so we could easily spot those who did not belong. Now our enemies' soldiers are hidden in street clothes and blend in without trouble in America's melting pot. These people are capable of killing themselves along with hundreds or even thousands of innocent bystanders, and, more important, they are ready and willing to do so with the sole purpose of inflicting terror, death, and destruction on our population as a means of retaliation, as they see it, against our government. It was our mission to find them and stop them before they carried out their plans, whatever those plans were. Unfortunately we didn't know when, where, or how they might attack, so we had to be ready for when—not if—they did.

Three

In July 1996, a year after the Allegiant Sentry 95 training, my thirty-two-member IBU-24 unit was deployed once again to Puerto Rico to undergo even more intensive two-week training with the US military's Special Operations Forces (SOF), an active and reserve component force with personnel from each branch of the military, each appointed specifically by the secretary of defense. SOF is highly organized, trained, and equipped to conduct and support a variety of specialized operations both domestic and foreign, some of which are highly classified and/or clandestine. Some are of a more mundane nature—providing support to local law-enforcement agencies during high-profile or high-risk occasions such as major sporting events (the Olympics, the World Cup) or political conventions—but are important nonetheless. Whenever large crowds of people converge, especially over highly charged topics like sports and politics, there is substantial risk of destruction, injury, and even domestic terrorism. The Special Forces make these situations as safe as possible for all who attend. In recent years, they have also been deployed to nations such as Pakistan, Afghanistan, Iraq, Somalia, and Yemen for operations including the hunt for Osama bin Laden, providing support to federal armies against militant groups, and targeting, as the

White House called them, individuals who pose "continuing and imminent threat to the American people."

Needless to say, it was an honor and a truly valuable learning experience to train with the SFO. While in Puerto Rico, we learned mostly about fighting tactics and weaponry of all types. We would start by examining a weapon's basic composition, which we discovered by breaking it down into pieces and putting it back together. This is called *field breaking*, and we learn it because if a weapon becomes jammed up while we're out on a mission (in the field), there won't be a gun shop anywhere around that we can take it to for repairs. It will need to be fixed on the spot, and we have to be the ones to do it. In order to gain this level of proficiency, we took apart each weapon in the SFO's arsenal and put it back together over and over again, to the point where we could accurately identify one small part in isolation from a larger weapon.

We were also drilled in weapon safety during this process—not just handling the weapon but knowing that it has been assembled properly, to avoid any malfunctions. Even if we witnessed the person next to us taking a weapon apart and putting it back together right in front of us, we had to do the same inspection ourselves to ensure the weapon was safe and that its chambers were empty. That's the level of detail at which the SFO operates.

Once we were well versed in weapon mechanics and safety, it was time to learn how to shoot. Every day we spent time at the fire lane, or firing range, shooting all the different weapons we had just learned to take apart and rebuild. We started small, with .45-caliber handguns, then moved on to the A1 rifle, the

```
                    DEPARTMENT OF THE NAVY
                      NAVAL RESERVE CENTER
                    FORT DIX, NJ  08640-0000

                                                    15 MAY 1996

FROM:  COMMANDING OFFICER, NAVAL RESERVE CENTER
TO:    EM2 TOMAS PIMENTAL           USN▓▓▓▓▓▓▓
       ▓▓ CARR AVE
       KEANSBURG, NJ  07734-1336

SUBJ:  COMNAVRESFOR SDN: N6899496RT00390
       DUTY IN CONNECTION WITH AT

REF:   (A) SEC 270, 271 OR 511, TITLE 10 USC
       (B) PUBLIC LAW 92426

                   ------ULTIMATE ACTIVITY------

BY THE AUTHORITY IN REFERENCE (A) OR (B) YOU ARE HEREBY ORDERED TO
PROCEED AND REPORT AS DIRECTED BELOW FOR A PERIOD OF 0012 DAYS
TO PERFORM AT WITH PAY, PLUS 2 TRAVEL DAYS.


REPORT NOT LATER THAN 0730 ON 15 JUL 1996         EDA: 15 JUL 1996
TO: COMMANDING OFFICER                            UIC: 55180
    NAVAL SPECIAL WARFARE UNIT 4
    BOX 3400
    FPO AA 34051-3400

       LOC ROOSEVELT ROADS PR
FOR AT
PERSONNEL ACCOUNTING SUPPORT: NAVSPECWARUNIT 4    UIC: 55180

UPON COMPLETION OF AT AND WHEN DIRECTED ON 26 JUL 1996 DETACH.

                   ------ACCOUNTING DATA------

AA  1761405.7210  011   00072   0   68518  2D  T00390  068994671600  0000101607
AD  1761405.7210  012   00072   0   68518  2D  T00390  068994671601  0000005687
AB  1761405.7210  021   00072   0   68518  2D  T00390  068994674600  0000003400
AC  1761405.7210  021   00072   0   68518  2D  T00390  068994674601  0000052788
AC  1761405.7210  021   00072   0   68518  1K  T00390  068994674601  ADVANCE AMT

TOTAL PAID LUMP SUM LEAVE DAYS ARE: 37
ALL COST OF PAY AND ALLOWANCES ARE CHARGEABLE TO RPN.
PAY GRADE/PEBD: E5 / 30 JUL 1987  BAQ W/D: Y    DATE REPORTED  JUL 1 3 1996
CSP: 03 Y 02 M 25 D
FLIGHT PAY AUTHORIZED: N                        DATE DEPARTED _____
                                                GOVERNMENT BERTHING   AVAILABLE/NOT AVAILABLE
This member is/is not physically qualified      GOVERNMENT MESSING    AVAILABLE/NOT AVAILABLE
for Annual Training/ADT
_____  13Ju196
Signature of Med. Dept. Rep.    Date
```

Military order to train with Special Forces.

M60 machine gun, the .50-caliber rifle (the quintessential sniper rifle), and at last the MK19 grenade launcher. We shot each of these weapons on land as well as mounted onboard a boat so we could feel and get used to the differences in stance, aiming, balance, and so on we would need to use in these different scenarios.

On the first day, with the .45 caliber, we shot at a target from twenty-five yards, then closed in on it, shooting at fifteen yards, ten yards, and five yards. We practiced close-combat weapon retention, or how to maintain possession and control of a weapon when in physical proximity to an assailant who is trying to grab hold of it.

When we shot the A1 rifle, we did so only from 300 yards out, a standard distance for usage of this weapon. We practiced different positions—prone, lying flat on the floor, standing, and kneeling—that would mimic any real-life scenarios in which we might have to utilize such a firearm. Last, we did all the M60, .50 caliber, and MK19 shooting from the boat, twelve miles out into international waters. These weapons are commonly used during operations at sea, particularly the MK19, which can neutralize all types of large machinery and even a big ship if needed. This would not likely have been necessary for us in the IBU-24, but we could have found ourselves at some point in a situation where we would have needed to engage with another vessel until more support arrived, so we did have to learn the techniques.

While we were on site with the Special Forces team in Puerto Rico, I also got to show off my electrical engineering expertise one day when a boat belonging to Port Security broke down. No one on the PS unit could repair it after several hours, so I stepped in to give it a shot. While troubleshooting the problem, I discovered that a cable had developed some resistance, preventing the electrical current from getting to the starter motor. We replaced the cable, and the boat was back in service.

At that point, Port Security took the boat back and gave us a junker on which to do our drills and exercises. We were out on that boat three days later, when the federal Drug Enforcement Agency (DEA) wanted to use us—IBU-24 and the SFO personnel who were training us—to intercept a boat that was already en route to Puerto Rico from the Dominican Republic. Allegedly it was full of drugs and illegal immigrants. That was all we heard about it though; the mission never came through, and we did not work with the DEA at that time.

At the end of this two-week training, we were ready to start working on whatever tasks the navy or federal government would assign to us. That came a few weeks after our return to New Jersey, when our CO asked for a volunteer to go to New York for our first mission. There would be no pay, as the budget for the year had been expended, and the new budget for the current period had not yet been approved. Instead, whoever stepped up to go would get to skip the next drill weekend. Unfortunately, no one in the unit seemed interested in that sort of trade-off. We'd been traveling and drilling a lot, and they wanted some time with their families.

I understood; yes, we had each been hand picked for this team because of our dedication to the navy and to our country, but that didn't mean we had no lives outside of our military service. We still had families and friends. We had homes to keep and jobs to attend to support ourselves; since our military service was part time, so was the pay we received for it. Don't get me wrong—I'm not looking for some sort of sympathy or to say that being a part of the IBU-24 was any sort of hardship. On the contrary, it was an honor, one of the highest of my life so far. And I know the other people in the unit felt the same.

Still, they couldn't bring themselves to volunteer for this extra work, not even with the delayed incentive of time off later. So I raised my hand. I wasn't trying to prove a point or take one for the team. I just felt it was our duty to serve in whatever capacity we were needed, and somebody had to fulfill this necessary mission. So, I figured that it might as well be me.

First, the CO told me to get in touch with BM1 (the Boatswain's Mate First Class, or the person who trains, directs, and supervises personnel on a ship) for the details of the mission. I did so and found out that I would need to go to New York City for a rendezvous with a CIA agent whom I would take around New York Harbor for some reconnaissance. The BM1 told me to report for duty just a few days later, on Friday, October 18, 1996, at Fort Dix, and from there we would go into the city. Normally, we would have gone on Saturday, but the BM1 knew there was always heavy traffic going into New York on the weekend, so we would leave one day ahead of schedule in order to miss it. Our berthing—our housing for the weekend—would be at Fort Wadsworth on Staten Island, New York, a former military base dating back to 1663. It had been closed in 1994 and was now a national park, and a former family housing unit from the base had been converted into two- and three-bedroom apartments where traveling military personnel could stay while in town for a mission.

That Friday, I arrived at the Pooka—the building at Fort Dix where my fellow reservists and I reported for duty on drill weekends—at 7:30 a.m. The BM1 was waiting for me with our set of military orders: We would leave at 4:30 p.m. and go to Fort Wadsworth for the night, and then on early on Saturday morning we would pick up the CIA agent to take him around the city. At the Pooka, we went to the transportation compound and hooked up a boat trailer to a truck. Then we did our safety check, making sure the blinkers and brakes worked well and so on. We did a pre-engineering checkup on the boat we would use as well to ensure it was in good working condition. Then we reviewed the route we would take to Staten Island so we would know where to go and hopefully arrive with no difficulties along the way.

Finally, we got the boat up onto the trailer we had hitched to the truck, and then we headed to the fuel yard to top off both. We exited the base at 4:45 p.m. and drove north on the New Jersey Turnpike. Around exit ten we began to see some traffic and for quite a while moved only about ten feet at a time and then stopped for long intervals. It was eight thirty by the time we got to Fort Wadsworth. The first thing we did was unhook the boat from the truck and drive out to get something to eat, as the cafeteria on the base was closed by then. Afterward, we scouted out a launching place for the boat; we found one right by the Verrazano Bridge and went back to Fort Wadsworth and turned in for the night.

The next morning, we got the boat in the water by eight thirty and met the CIA agent at ten o'clock at the dock where

```
                    DEPARTMENT OF THE NAVY
                    NAVAL RESERVE CENTER
                    FORT DIX, NJ   08640-0000
                                                        02 OCT 1996
FROM:   COMMANDING OFFICER, NAVAL RESERVE CENTER
TO:     EM2 TOMAS PIMENTAL            USNR
            CARR AVE
        KEANSBURG, NJ   07734-1336

SUBJ:   COMNAVRESFOR SDN: N6833197RW12033
        DUTY IN CONNECTION WITH IDTT

REF:    (A) JOINT FEDERAL TRAVEL REGULATION (JFTR)

                ------ULTIMATE ACTIVITY------

BY THE AUTHORITY IN REFERENCE (A) YOU ARE HEREBY DIRECTED TO
PROCEED AND REPORT AS DIRECTED BELOW FOR A PERIOD OF 0003 DAYS
TO PERFORM IDTT IN NON-PAY STATUS, PLUS 0 TRAVEL DAY.

REPORT NOT LATER THAN 0730 ON 18 OCT 1996           EDA: 18 OCT 1996
TO: OFFICER IN CHARGE                               UIC: 47117
    INSHORE BOAT UNIT 24
    FORT DIX, NJ   08204-7800

UPON COMPLETION OF IDTT AND WHEN DIRECTED ON 20 OCT 1996 DETACH.

                ------ACCOUNTING DATA------

YOU ARE DIRECTED TO OBTAIN PROPER ENDORSEMENTS FOR CHECKIN, CHECKOUT AND
QUARTERS / MESSING AVAILABILITY.

THE JOINT FEDERAL TRAVEL REGULATIONS, VOLUME 1, ALLOWS 10 CALENDAR DAYS
TO FILE A TRAVEL CLAIM, HOWEVER, TO ENSURE MAXIMUM UTILIZATION OF FUNDS,
UNEXECUTED ORDERS AND TRAVEL CLAIMS MUST BE COMPLETED IMMEDIATELY UPON
COMPLETION OF IDTT AND FORWARDED IN ONE PACKAGE TO THE IDTT OPTAR HOLDER.
```

Military order to take the CIA agent around NYC, to study the landscape to prevent terrorist attacks.

the Staten Island Ferry picked up and dropped off passengers. This would be the rally point, or the starting point for the mission; from there we would navigate around the city so the agent could observe and take pictures of the landscape and skyline of New York and particular sites of interest, such as the Statue of Liberty, the World Trade Center, and the United Nations—all places that terrorists might want to target and exploit.

First, per the agent's request, we headed up the East River, up past Yankee Stadium and the nearby Macombs Dam (aka 155th Street) Bridge, which connects Manhattan and the Bronx. It was a slow ride so he could see what he needed to see and take pictures along the way. Meanwhile, I was enjoying the view of New York City from the boat. It's one thing to see it from New Jersey on the other side of the Hudson River, but it's entirely another to be *on* the river looking up at what some consider to be the greatest city in the world. Everything seemed so much bigger when we were that close to it.

After the bridge, we turned around and headed back down the river, toward Randall's Island. The agent asked us occasionally to slow down; for example, when we reached the area of the United Nations building and at the Twin Towers. There, he actually had us stop, and he looked around for a while. Last, we made a slow trip around Liberty Island off the end of Manhattan. It was amazing to see Lady Liberty so close, right from the water. I just stared while the agent took photo after photo.

That drew our tour of the east side of Manhattan to a close. Next, we went up the west side along the Hudson River, passing the George Washington Bridge and then going back down to the lower section of the island. By 3:00 p.m. the CIA agent had gotten all the information he needed, so we dropped him off back at the rally point. With our mission completed, the BM1 and I rode around New York Harbor to do a little sightseeing as well as some maneuver training. After a couple of hours, we went back to the launch near the Verrazano, got the boat out of the water, and headed back to the Coast Guard station. We stayed on the base for one more night and returned to Fort Dix on Sunday morning.

Though this mission was a fairly enjoyable one, it was still serious business. At that time, the federal government had many leads on terrorist activities that might take place, but there were no definite dates, times, or locations. Of course they always figured any terrorist group would go for one of the United States' national monuments or other places of cultural significance, economic or military importance, and so on. These types of sites abound in New York, and, on top of that, the city's dense population is attractive to terrorists. The more damage they can do at once, the better they believe it is for their cause.

It was also believed that terrorists might target Jewish neighborhoods in Brooklyn because they—the terrorists—believe the worldwide Jewish community controls all international commerce, in particular the World Trade Center, which was a hub of international business. (Which was, in turn, why they had tried to topple the towers in 1993.) The terrorists also claimed the United States helped the Jews to oppress the Palestinians through our ongoing aid to Israel, and as long as we continued that, no Americans would sleep peacefully.

At that point, the CIA, FBI, and military intelligence thought that al-Qaeda or another terrorist group would attack the United States on a major holiday, again for the cultural significance of casting a dark shadow over a day that should be joyous for many Americans. This prediction had first been floated prior to Christmas 1999, the last Christmas in the millennium, but thankfully that did not come to pass. Nor were there any incidents on Christmas 2000 (significant because it was the first Christmas of the millennium) or on July Fourth of that same year.

For that holiday, our whole unit went into New York to provide security from June 25 through July 7. The Fourth is always a big day for partying and being outdoors, and that year, like everything else, it was a millennial celebration, so everything was expected to be bigger and louder than ever before. New York City over that weekend would have been a perfect place for a terrorist group to strike, so the entire IBU-24 unit was sent in to monitor and protect the city's landmarks. The problem was we were not allowed to bring in any weapons with us; the mayor at the time, Rudy Giuliani, did not want the city to look like a war zone. So all we could do was keep other boats away from the Statue of Liberty and the Twin Towers. Fortunately, nothing out of the ordinary happened, and everyone enjoyed the historic holiday.

Based on the intelligence the federal government had collected, and the CIA's, FBI's, and military intelligence's ongoing vigilance in monitoring and policing known and potential terrorists, they had concluded any attack that might take place would be carried out with missiles or bombs, as they would be the least complicated to deliver and have the biggest payoff. In other words, they would create the most damage and injure or kill the most US citizens.

Another theory was that some terrorists might take advantage of what was known at the time as the Y2K bug. This had to do with a set of problems existing in computer systems prior to January 1, 2000. The main issue was that dates—specifically years—had always been represented in computer systems and software by two digits, not four. For example, 1996 would be just 96. The problem with this was that when the year rolled over from 1999 to 2000, computers might not recognize it as a linear increase because it would not have the first two digits. To a computer it would just be 00, which—or so people hypothesized—could be interpreted as 1900 instead.

This, of course, would cause all kinds of problems (again, hypothetically) as computers run so much of our modern lives. Each computer, big or small, has a clock built into its hardware that runs at all times (even when the machine is off) and passes time and date information to any software used on the system. The problem—the Y2K bug—was that most dates up to that point had been entered as two digits (96 for 1996), but most PCs calculated dates only in four-digit years (1996). What was more, most programs automatically expanded two-digit years to four digits but made assumptions about what century the user intended. That is, we could enter "00" for 2000, but the software could interpret it as 1900. In this way, the data becomes incorrect in a way that might not be apparent to the user, and any data generated by, for example, accounting, spreadsheet, scheduling, or payroll software, to name a few, could not be trusted to be correct. It should be obvious how such errors could affect many aspects of our day-to-day lives, to say nothing of the mission-critical software our military and defense systems depend upon to carry out their operations. Entire long-working systems across many fields of business and society could have broken down when the date-numbering process broke down suddenly, as it ascended from 99 to 00.

So how might a terrorist group use this Y2K bug to its advantage? Basically, it would use the chaos such a situation might produce to its advantage. There were many suppositions and rumors about what might happen when the clock struck midnight on December 31, 1999. Some people withdrew all their money from banks prior to then because they believed they would lose access to it due to the Y2K bug, or that it would simply disappear. Others wondered (happily, I imagine) what would happen to their student loan or credit card debts if the computer systems that kept track of them suddenly did not work. Some people even believed the Y2K bug would cause missiles to launch by themselves, inadvertently starting a third world war.

And if any of this did come to pass, the terrorists would be ready. While our authorities would undoubtedly be trying to quell the chaos that would ensue, any terrorist organization could slip under the radar, so to speak, and perhaps carry out those attacks we'd been suspecting for years. Because of this, New Year's Eve 1999 was a high-security date, and the IBU-24 trained accordingly in the lead-up to the end of the year. We brought the Coast Guard in to once again train us in the protocols of stopping, boarding, and searching boats for illegal weapons and contraband. We once again trained in weapon retention, which even included subjecting ourselves to pepper spray so we would know what to do if it was used against us in an attack. Those days and nights were never ending, but our unit was indefatigable, as all of the US military was and remains to this day when it comes to terrorism.

Photos taken during antiterrorism work during June and July 2000 in NYC.

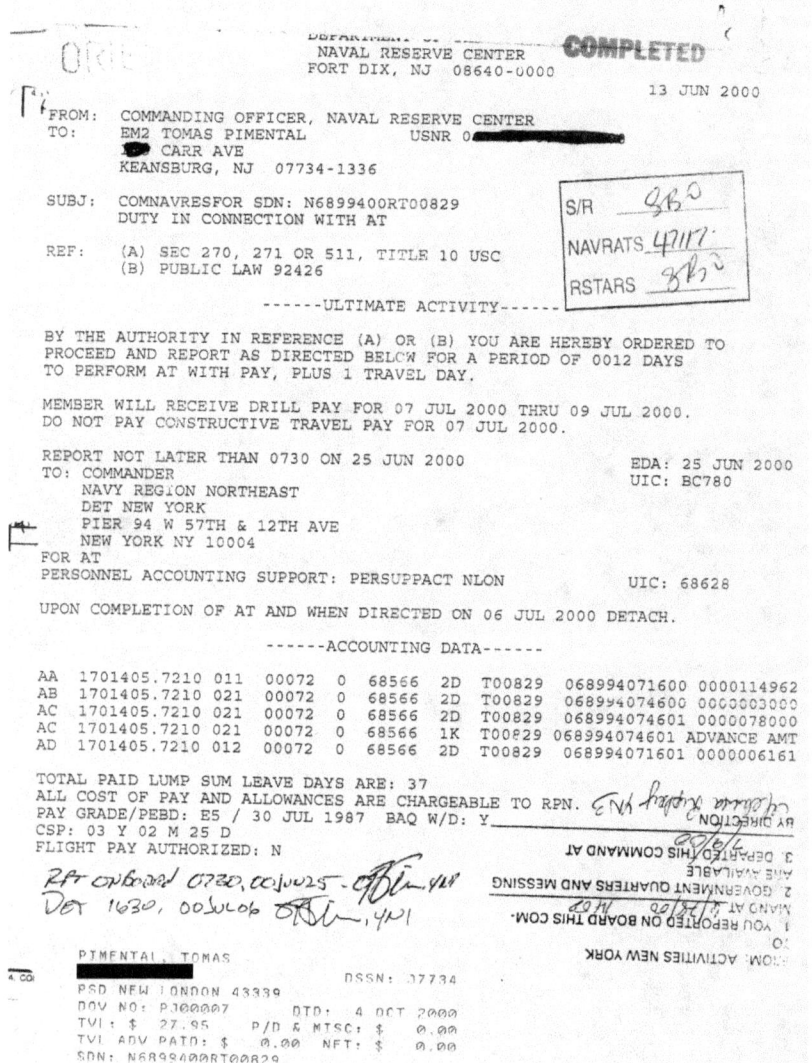

Military order to provide security around NYC, to prevent terrorist attacks.

Photos taken during antiterrorism work during June and July 2000 in NYC.

Four

Even in what was considered peacetime, the IBU-24 unit remained ever vigilant. Whether a terrorist attack took place or not, we stood guard around New York City, regularly patrolling the rivers and the harbor, looking for anything amiss or out of place in the vicinities of the major monuments and buildings. Fortunately, we never saw anything, and no major events occurred.

Things were not so peaceful, however, in other areas of the world. As there has been for so many years, there was great unrest in the Middle East at the turn of the century, and the United States held a constant presence in many nations that either needed our help in protecting themselves against insurgent attacks; were insurgent themselves; or actively participating in the oppression of and violence against neighboring countries, minorities within their own countries, and so on. Sometimes we even had to (and still have to) protect a nation's people from their own government, when their leaders become despots and tyrants bent on gaining ultimate power.

The issues at stake in the area are vast and deep-seated; they are complex enough to fill an entire book, and have done just that many times over. Regardless of the historical reasons and the present-day disagreements that have brought our military to the Middle East, the important fact is that we are there, standing vigilant and keeping the peace however we can.

It was in this capacity that the navy's USS *Cole* was deployed on August 8, 2000. For several months, it spent most of its time in the Mediterranean and Adriatic Seas, but in October it was sent toward Yemen, an Arab country at the southern end of the Arabian Peninsula, just below Saudi Arabia. The USS *Cole* stayed anchored in the waters outside of Aden, a seaport in Yemen, where the guided-missile destroyer was to refuel. This was a routine stop; they harbored at about nine thirty in the morning, and the refueling started an hour later.

Forty-five minutes into the task, much of the crew of the USS *Cole* were just lining up in the galley for lunch. At the same time, up on the decks, someone spotted a small craft approaching the ship on the port side. This was unexpected; any contact they had with the fueling vessels had already been established. Before anyone on the destroyer could follow the protocol for such a situation, however, an explosion occurred, ripping a forty-by-forty-foot hole in the *Cole*'s side—and right into the galley.

Immediately, the destroyer began to flood. Those who had not been injured in the blast set to fighting the influx of seawater, especially in the engineering areas of the ship. It took three days to bring the ship back to a safe state. But by that time, the damage had been done: In all, seventeen sailors had been killed in the attack, and thirty-nine more had been injured. These statistics made this the deadliest attack against a US naval vessel since 1987, during the Iran-Iraq war, when Iraqi aircraft fired upon the USS *Stark*, an American naval guided-missile frigate. That ship was part of the Middle East

Task Force at the time. The Iraqi pilot attacked with two 1,500-pound Exocet missiles that the *Stark*'s crew could not see coming until seconds before the impact. The first did not detonate, but its fuel ignited a fire on the port side hull that raged for twenty-four hours. The second missile also struck the port side, and this one exploded, leaving a ten-by-fifteen-foot hole. In total, thirty-seven sailors were killed (two of which were lost at sea) and twenty-one were wounded.

In the case of the *Cole*, which was not engaged in any war arena at the time of the attack, people wanted to know who had undertaken this evil deed and, most important, why. But no claims were forthcoming at the time. It wouldn't be until June 2001 that we would hear the first acknowledgment of responsibility, when Osama bin Laden boasted about the attack on the USS *Cole* in an al-Qaeda recruitment video. He also urged his followers to carry out similar violent acts.

Long before that admission of guilt, however, the USS *Cole* situation had been a wake-up call for the US Navy. Not that we had been sleeping before; exactly the opposite, we were always on high alert no matter where in the world we served, domestically or abroad. However, after this attack in Yemen, we had to focus our attention on that area more than ever, and toward that end the priorities for my unit, the IBU-24, changed as well. Though our assignment had always been to provide protection and surveillance around the island of Manhattan, New York, now we were going to be deployed to the Middle East, to provide protection for our troops who were already embedded there. Specifically, we went to Dubai, and we were stationed there from December 20, 2000, through April 29, 2001. We were also deployed to other areas from May 2002 until September 2002, from February 2003 until June 2003, and from July 2004 until May 2005. However, I cannot discuss the details of what any of these assignments entailed or what my responsibilities within them were. All of the missions we undertook at that time were, understandably, of a highly classified nature. But they were all under the umbrella of performing antiterrorism work for the US Navy.

By the time my unit and I returned to the United States in April 2001, after that first deployment to Dubai, the intelligence community here was expressing great concern that an attack on the nation might be imminent. They were picking up and intercepting a lot of communication between known terrorists and terrorist organizations overseas—none of it exactly specific but enough to raise some alarms and put us all on high alert. Based on the information our communications experts were able to glean, it was believed some act of terrorism would take place in July of that year, at either the World Trade Center (also called the Twin Towers for its two main original structures, each of which stood at almost 1,400 feet, making them the tallest buildings in the world) or the Statue of Liberty.

These were sites my unit and I had guarded before, and we knew them well. We'd spent hours, days, and weeks patrolling the East and Hudson Rivers, one on either side of Manhattan. Day in and day out we would follow the same route, scanning the skyline and the shore below it, looking for any activity that seemed suspicious. This time, we would not be deployed to stand guard over these landmarks, as our boats and weapons were still overseas awaiting transport back to our home base at Fort Dix. That doesn't mean they were left vulnerable; of

Photos taken while deployed for antiterrorism work in the Middle East.

DEPARTMENT OF THE NAVY
BUREAU OF NAVAL PERSONNEL
MILLINGTON, TN 38055

09DEC00

FROM: CHIEF OF NAVAL PERSONNEL
TO: NAVAL RESERVE CENTER FORT DIX 5951 NEWPORT ST. FORT DIX, NJ 08640
SUBJ: BUPERS ORDERS 0005
OFFICIAL RECALL TO ACTIVE DUTY ORDER FOR
EM2 THOMAS PIMENTEL
___ CARR AVENUE
KEANSBURG, NJ 07734

REF: (A) SEC 12304, TITLE 10 USC
(B) COMNAVRESFOR NEW ORLEANS LA 081315ZDEC00
(C) MOBILIZATION EVENT NBR: 402
(D) OPNAVINST 3060.7A
(E) ITEMPO NAVADMIN 255/00
(F) CURRENT CNO N1 POLICY AND GUIDANCE MSG ISO OPERATIONS IN AND AROUND SOUTHWEST ASIA.

XXXXXXXXXXXXXXXXXXXXXXXXXXXXXXXXXXXXXXXXXXXXXXXXXXXXXXXXXXXXXXX
IN CARRYING OUT/PROCESSING THESE ORDERS, ALL SECTIONS
MUST BE READ AND LISTED INSTRUCTIONS COMPLIED WITH
XXXXXXXXXXXXXXXXXXXXXXXXXXXXXXXXXXXXXXXXXXXXXXXXXXXXXXXXXXXXXXX

------ACTIVATION ACTIVITY------

BY THE AUTHORITY IN REFERENCES (A) THROUGH (D) YOU ARE HEREBY INVOLUNTARILY ORDERED TO REPORT FOR ACTIVE DUTY, IN SUPPORT OF OPERATIONS IN AND AROUND SOUTHWEST ASIA FOR UP TO 270 DAYS FROM DATE ORDERED UNLESS RELEASED BY COMPETENT AUTHORITY. REPORT AS DIRECTED BELOW FOR ACTIVATION.

REPORT NOT EARLIER THAN 0730 ON 09DEC00
BUT NOT LATER THAN 0800 ON 09DEC00   EDA: 09DEC00
TO NRC FORT DIX NJ   UIC: 68994
LOCATION: FORT DIX, NJ 08640
FOR TEMPORARY DUTY   ACC: 103
PERSONNEL ACCOUNTING SUPPORT PSD WILLOW GROVE PA   UIC: 43315

------MOBILIZATION ACTIVITY------

UPON COMPLETION OF ACTIVATION, INITIAL DELAY AND EXEMPTION PROCESSING, REPORT AS DIRECTED BELOW, TO THE NAVY MOBILIZATION PROCESSING SITE (NMPS) FOR MOBILIZATION TO ACTIVE DUTY. IF FOUND NOT PHYSICALLY QUALIFIED, RETURN TO THE ABOVE ACTIVATION SITE FOR DEACTIVATION AND RETURN TO HOME ADDRESS. UPON ARRIVAL AT HOME ADDRESS, YOU ARE CONSIDERED RELEASED FROM ACTIVE DUTY. AUTHORIZED SPECIAL CONVEYANCE IF MEMBER MEETS CRITERIA IN REF (F).

REPORT ON OR ABOUT 11DEC00   EDA: 11DEC00
TO COMNAVREG MIDLANT   UIC: 61463
LOCATION: NORFOLK, VA
FOR TEMPORARY DUTY   ACC: 103
PERSONNEL ACCOUNTING SUPPORT: PSD NAVSTA NORFOLK, VA   UIC: 42574

------INTERMEDIATE ACTIVITY------

UPON COMPLETION OF ACTIVATION, INITIAL DELAY AND EXEMPTION PROCESSING, REPORT AS DIRECTED BELOW, TO THE NAVY MOBILIZATION PROCESSING SITE (NMPS) FOR MOBILIZATION TO ACTIVE DUTY. IF FOUND NOT PHYSICALLY QUALIFIED, RETURN TO THE ABOVE ACTIVATION SITE FOR DEACTIVATION AND RETURN TO HOME ADDRESS. UPON ARRIVAL AT HOME ADDRESS, YOU ARE CONSIDERED RELEASED FROM ACTIVE DUTY.

Military order to go to the Middle East to do antiterrorism work due to the attack on the USS *Cole*.

REPORT ON OR ABOUT ___13DEC00___   EDA: ___13DEC00___
TO: ___COMNCWGRU TWO___   UIC: ___62638___
LOCATION: ___WILLIAMSBURG, VA___
FOR TEMPORARY DUTY   ACC: ___103___
PERSONNEL ACCOUNTING SUPPORT: ___PSD LITTLE CREEK NORFOLK, VA___   UIC: ___42575___

------ULTIMATE ACTIVITY------

UPON COMPLETION OF INTERMEDIATE PROCESSING/TRAINING AND AS DIRECTED BELOW REPORT TO ULTIMATE DUTY STATION FOR DUTY. FOR PAY AND PERSONNEL ACCOUNTING REPORT TO PERSONNEL SUPPORT ACTIVITY DETACHMENT AS INDICATED BELOW:

REPORT ON OR ABOUT ___16DEC00___   EDA: ___16DEC00___
TO: ___COMNCWGRU TWO DET B___   UIC: ___62638___
LOCATION ___UAE___   ACC: ___103___
FOR ACTIVE DUTY
PERSONNEL ACCOUNTING SUPPORT: ___PSD LITTLE CREEK NORFOLK, VA___   UIC: ___42575___
DETACH NOT LATER THAN: ___22JUL01___   SPI: ___1___
                                         BSC: ___N/A___

PARA/ LINE NUMBER_____SWE-00114_____

------DEMOBILIZATION PROCESS------

UPON COMPLETION OF DUTY AND WHEN DIRECTED, DETACH IN ACCORDANCE WITH **THE DETACH NOT LATER THAN DATE** TO PERMIT SEPARATION PROCESSING, AUTHORIZED LEAVE AND ALLOWED TRAVEL TIME BEFORE EXPIRATION OF ACTIVE SERVICE OF 270 DAYS MOBILIZATION. IF APPLICABLE, REPORT TO CPC/CRC PRIOR TO REPORTING TO YOUR NAVY MOBILIZATION PROCESSING SITE (NMPS). REPORT TO THE NAVY MOBILIZATION PROCESSING SITE (NMPS) WHEN DIRECTED, DETACH AND PROCEED TO YOUR NAVAL RESERVE ACTIVITY (NRA) FOR DEMOBILIZATION PROCESSING. UPON ARRIVAL AT HOME ADDRESS YOU ARE CONSIDERED RELEASED FROM ACTIVE DUTY.

------ACCOUNTING DATA------

(A) FROM HOME TO PERMANENT DUTY STATION AND RETURN

ENLISTED
ACCESSION ACCOUNTING DATA:
NKL1 1711453.2250 F 000022 AV KL1/1/9/5 KL1

SEPARATION ACCOUNTING DATA:
NNI 11711453.2254 F 000022 AV NI1/1/9/W NI1

(B) PAY AND ALLOWANCES (All cost of pay and allowances are chargeable to MPN):

ENLISTED: 1711453.2202 12600 2D 000000071148

(C) PER DIEM: COMNAVPERSCOM Operations and Maintenance, Navy (O&M,N) accounting data is to be used for per diem charges for Reservists recalled under PRC in support of operations in and around Southwest Asia:

N6298001TOTE508AA 1711804.22C0 000 62980 0 068892 2D 1TE508629801TE910E

PAY GRADE/PEBD: ___E5/30JUL87___

------SPECIAL INSTRUCTIONS------

course other protective measures were put into effect. It was just that the IBU-24 would be sitting this one out.

Still, I followed what was going on in and around the city. It was no surprise to me that these places were once again being targeted or that the threats against them were, as usual, somewhat vague. One of the most insidious aspects of terrorism, at least as it has been perpetrated against the United States, is that you never know what form it will take. We had trained and were prepared for a variety of different scenarios: air attacks in which planes would drop bombs or missiles on the city, attacks via water in which a boatload of explosives could dock somewhere in the city and create great damage with a single detonation, and even land-based attacks in which, for example, a lone suicide bomber with a charge of C4 strapped to his midsection could infiltrate a crowd of spectators at the city's July Fourth fireworks show and blow himself up, taking potentially thousands of innocent New Yorkers with him.

There were—and are—countless scenarios when it comes to terrorism. People who conspire to commit such acts are, though we might hate to admit it, intelligent individuals. Often they are one or more steps ahead of those they aim to attack, as they must be if they want to take that person, entity, or nation down. One of the keys to successful terrorism is the element of surprise; a terrorist must be able to infiltrate the target unseen in order to remain anonymous, avoid detection, and wreak the most damage. This model has been proven effective time and time again, even on American soil, where we are always vigilant. Unfortunately, it's just not possible to foresee every potential action a terrorist might take.

But that doesn't mean we don't try, or that we simply throw

our hands up in the air and wait for an attack to happen. Even at the smallest hint of a brewing plot, even at the slightest detection of a threat, even when the information is vague or incomplete, our military and our government take it all seriously, and our armed forces are alerted and deployed to wherever they are needed. I've written it before here, but I will say it again and again: America does not sleep. Not when it comes to terrorism. So many people see only what happens on the surface or what they are shown on the nightly news, and when a terrorist act comes to its terrible fruition, these individuals are quick to ask, "Well, where was our government? Where were our armed forces? Why didn't they know? Why didn't they stop it before it happened?"

These are all good and important questions to ask. We have many freedoms as US citizens, including our rights to demand information, to question authority, and to speak our minds. These are freedoms that, as a member of the US military, I defend and fight for every day.

However, I do not and cannot defend those people who use such questions to incite fear and hatred of our elected leaders and our armed forces. People like this ask the questions but never seem satisfied with the replies, which is unfair because there *are* answers to all these questions.

Where was our government? In Washington, DC, and countries around the world, keeping tabs on known terrorists—watching all the moves they made, collecting information, creating profiles, and tracking activities over time, and then putting all those pieces together into coherent narratives that told the stories of where the terrorists might go next.

Where were our armed forces? Guarding our shores, our

land, and our airspace, and operating in many, many other nations where our presence could help protect the American public from terrorism.

Why didn't we know? As I've already written, we can't know everything. We find out as much as we can, and we actively pursue information in order to keep the people of the United States as safe as possible at all times. There is no stone we leave unturned, no clue we leave uninvestigated, no tip we don't follow through on. The government and the military's war on terrorism is thorough and never ending, and it goes much, much deeper than it appears to the average person. Still, there are some things in life that no one can predict no matter how informed and prepared they are.

The last question—"Why didn't we stop it before it happened?"—is one I've heard quite often, especially since September 2001. And I understand why people want to know. Whenever any great tragedy or trauma occurs, even if it's just on a small, personal scale, we want to be able to blame someone for it. Not to be vindictive or hateful but just because assigning responsibility for things that are so overwhelming helps us make sense of them. It gives us a target on which to focus our energies and emotions; it gives us someone or something to hold accountable so we don't have to wonder if there is anything we could have done differently ourselves to have prevented it.

This is a normal reaction for any human being. It's unlikely that any one person could have stopped the terrorist attacks of September 11, 2001, but we all still wonder, "What if?" What if you had taken a different train that day, had called out sick, had not stopped for coffee? Where would you have been? How would your experience of that day have changed—for worse or for better? We can't answer that question; we simply can't know, and the frustration of that only adds to our fear. Seeking others to blame, then, is an innate attempt on our part to try to sublimate the terror we feel.

But is this a good excuse for blind disbelief in the forces that protect us and our country? Of course it's not. Just because you can't see it doesn't mean it's not happening or it's not there—the same as it is with terrorism. You might not see soldiers walking the streets or hear your representatives in DC giving weekly speeches about the many ways in which they are fighting and winning the war on terror, but none of that indicates that nothing is being done. It simply means that in the big machine that is our military and governmental complex, there are way too many things happening, more than we could ever make the public aware. But trust me, they are happening. I know because I have been a part of them.

Five

No terrorist attack occurred in New York City in July 2001. The World Trade Center and the Statue of Liberty remained safe at that time. Nothing out of the ordinary occurred; thankfully, whatever the terrorists in question had been planning did not come to pass. My unit, and indeed all of the military personnel in the area, remained on high alert as always, and we continued to patrol the waters around Manhattan as necessary. And, of course, we continued our three days of drilling a month, so we could keep our skills and ourselves in shape and our team ready to go in case of emergency. Remember: Once called, we had only twenty-four hours to report for duty.

Despite our vigilance, however, the terrorists finally did get through. On September 11, 2001, a series of coordinated attacks were carried out in New York City and Washington, DC, viciously murdering almost three thousand people and damaging or destroying $10 billion in property. Islamic terrorist group al-Qaeda—the one the US military and government had been suspiciously tracking for so long—took credit for the atrocity. Despite all we had done, they managed to carry out their plan and bring it to its devastating fruition.

However, none of that is news now. We all lived through it; we all know what happened on that most terrible day in US history. We watched in horror as American Airlines flight 11, a passenger airline carrying seventy-six passengers, eleven crew members, and five hijackers slammed into the World Trade Center's North Tower at 8:46 a.m. As flames and smoke blazed and billowed from the buildings, people on the streets and on TV looked on in mute horror, aghast at this apparent accident that had befallen their city. It was only seventeen minutes later, when another plane—United Airlines flight 175, with fifty-one passengers, nine crew, and five hijackers aboard—flew into the South Tower, that we all understood this was no accident. This was on purpose. The United States was under attack.

Thirty minutes after the second impact, our collective attention was drawn to Arlington County, Virginia, where a third plane—American Airlines flight 77, with fifty-three passengers, six crew, and five hijackers—had slammed into the low-lying Pentagon building, leaving a massive, stark crater in its wake. Security cameras showed that the impact was so fast, so unexpected, it was almost not even caught on film; we can see the nose of the plane coming into frame, then a streak of bright light, then an enormous, deep-orange fireball erupts from the building. This would make it seem as though the plane was going at full speed or near to it as it dove into the side of the Pentagon. All aboard the plane were killed along with 125 people on the ground. Only a few minutes after this, the Federal Aviation Association (FAA) grounded all domestic aircraft and told all planes that were already in the air to land immediately.

However, one passenger plane did not comply: United Airlines flight 93, but only because it had been hijacked. Several passengers called their loved ones from the in-flight phones, and as they did so they learned about the fates of the other three planes that morning in New York and Virginia. Knowing they were probably next in whatever this evil conspiracy would turn out to be, a group of passengers rushed the cockpit, intending, it is believed, to overtake the hijackers. Among them was a thirty-two-year-old man named Todd Beamer, whose name has become synonymous with the colloquialism "let's roll"— the last words a GTE phone operator heard him say before he and the rest of the group enacted their heroic feat.

Beamer's story is exemplary of many that came out of these terrorist attacks—he could have or even should have been somewhere else, but a series of choices and events unwittingly put him in the wrong place at the wrong time. Todd had just returned from a family vacation to Italy the previous night and had the option to leave on a business trip to San Francisco that night or wait until the next morning. Wanting to spend a little more time with his two children and his wife, who was expecting their third child in January 2002, he opted to stay home and catch a flight out of Newark International Airport early on September 11, 2001.

The plane Todd Beamer boarded—United flight 93—was scheduled for takeoff at eight o'clock that morning but was delayed due to runway traffic for forty-two minutes. Only six minutes after it took to the sky, American Airlines flight 11 crashed into the North Tower of the World Trade Center; fifteen minutes later, United flight 175 hit the South Tower. No one on Todd's plane knew anything about these events, and their plane kept climbing.

All seemed well with United flight 93 for the first half hour or so. The plane reached its cruising altitude; the pilot turned off the seatbelt signs, and the flight attendants were preparing to make their first passes with the drink carts. In total the flight was supposed to take six hours, and all the passengers were settling in—getting out their books and laptops, looking for extra blankets, chatting with their seatmates about the purposes of their trips. Many were heading out to the West Coast on business, just like Todd Beamer.

At 9:25 a.m., as United flight 93 flew over eastern Ohio, its pilot radioed the Cleveland air controllers, saying an alert was flashed on his cockpit computer: "Beware of cockpit intrusion." Unsure what it was about, the pilot left his mic on and tried to find out. Three minutes later, the controllers heard the sounds of a disturbance and screaming in the plane's cockpit. Three hijackers, led by a man later identified as Ziad Samir Jarrah, had forced their way in, killed the pilot and copilot, and taken control of the plane.

"Keep remaining sitting," Jarrah said to the passengers over the plane's intercom system. "We have a bomb onboard."

At that point, the hijackers drew open the curtains between the first and business class sections so they could herd everyone in the cabin toward the back of the plane. While being moved, Beamer got a glimpse toward the front and saw the bodies of the pilot and copilot lying on the floor outside the cockpit. A flight attendant who saw him looking said the hijackers had slit their throats. They had also killed a passenger in the same fashion.

By only nine minutes into the hijacking, the terrorists responsible for the act had taken control of the plane and everyone on it. At this point, thinking only that there was a bomb on the plane, as Jarrah had said, many passengers began phoning their loved ones. In those conversations, they learned about the World Trade Center and what their fate most likely would be. Todd Beamer was among those trying to use the in-flight phones, but he did not reach his wife; instead, his call was routed over the congested lines to a GTE airphone customer service representative, who passed the call on to a supervisor. There were also FBI agents listening in on the call.

With his quick description of the situation on the plane—three hijackers with knives, one with what appeared to be a bomb strapped around his waist, and two pilots and one passenger dead—Beamer provided the outside world with the best account we have of how exactly the terrorist acts committed on United flight 93 occurred. While he was on the phone with the operator, the hijackers banked the jet sharply south.

"We're going down! We're going down!" he shouted, his voice sounding understandably panicked.

But it was not to happen yet. The hijacker pilot righted the plane and continued on, now fully turned around and heading east, and the passengers were given a reprieve. In that moment, Todd Beamer and several other passengers formulated a plan to take back the plane and subdue the hijackers—to, as Todd told the phone operator, storm the cockpit, take over the plane, and drive it into the ground before these terrorists could carry out whatever their plan was.

Did they believe they could save themselves in this way? Or did they see it as their chance to save others, like those now fighting for their lives in the World Trade Center, from a certain and terrible demise? Though we have transcripts of all those inflight calls as well as cell phone data and the plane's black box, recovered after the crash, their intention will never be entirely clear. What is evident, though, is that they knew there was the possibility they would not make it out alive: Before heading to the cockpit to take on the hijackers, Todd Beamer led the GT representative and his fellow passengers in reciting the Lord's Prayer and the Twenty-Third Psalm.

"If I don't make it," he told the operator when he was done, "please call my family and let them know how much I love them."

Then he simply turned to the three other men who had volunteered to undertake this mission with him—Mark Bingham, Tom Burnett, and Jeremy Glick—and said those words that are now synonymous with the heroism of this day: "Are you ready? Okay. Let's roll."

What ensued is known only from the airplane's voice data recorder, recovered later. The men pounded against the cockpit door with their fists and their bodies and whatever they could, trying to get it open. There was shouting on both sides:

"Let's get them!" a passenger cried in English.

And in the cockpit: "Allahu akbar," an Islamic phrase in the Arabic language meaning "God is the greatest."

Jarrah, who was at the plane's controls, pitched the plane to and fro, trying to knock whoever was trying to get to him off their feet. But it didn't work. Todd Beamer and his cohorts continued to assail the cockpit door until finally they gained access. As they spilled in, one of them shouted, "In the cockpit! If we don't, we'll die!"

"Pull it down! Pull it down!" one of the hijackers commanded; we can assume he meant the nose of the plane, either to right the jet or to send it into a dive to the ground. Then the controls were turned hard to the right. The plane rolled onto its back, descended at 580 miles per hour, and crashed in an open field near Shanksville, Pennsylvania at just after 10:00 a.m. The jet hit the ground with such force and velocity, the only remnants of it were in bits and pieces, and all thirty-three passengers and seven crew, plus the four hijackers, were killed. Later, when a thorough investigation had been completed, it was believed that flight 93 had been heading for either the Capitol building or the White House in Washington, DC. It would have reached its destination in twenty minutes.

Though all these events—the planes crashing into the World Trade Center and the Pentagon, and the hijacking and destruction of flight 93—were happening along a timeline, they were orchestrated so that people in one place did not always know what was happening somewhere else. Thanks to the day and age in which we live, information traveled quickly, but it was not always accurate, and much confusion and fear remained. Who had done these terrible things? Was there more to come? What city would be hit next? People watched the skies in dread and anticipation, waiting for another plane to drop out of the sky.

All we could do was wait and wonder, and in that, perhaps, one could say that the terrorists fulfilled their goal: They had made us scared, fearful, and unsure of who we could trust or if we were really safe in the places we had always considered our homes. When terrorism is used as a political tool, this is the aim: to make the populace afraid of the enemy and untrusting of its own government, which they will see as failing to protect them. This is a fallacy, of course, but we will look at that issue a little later on.

In the meantime, the World Trade Center still burned. Medical professionals on the ground aided people who had been scorched by burning jet fuel coming from the sky, who had been hit by debris, and who had been injured in the mad push to get down the crowded stairwells inside the buildings. More than two thousand members of the New York Police Department and the Port Authority, both on duty and off, tried to get people away from the World Trade Center campus and keep them at a safe distance while the city's firefighters suited up and ran right into the burning buildings themselves, no questions asked. For a standard fire call, a department normally deploys three engines, two ladders, and a battalion chief along with the fighters themselves; a five-alarm fire calls for forty-four units.

The September 11 attacks on the World Trade Center constituted five five-alarm calls at once. More than 214 FDNY units responded with 112 engines, fifty-eight ladder trucks, five rescue companies, seven squad companies, four marine units, and multiple chiefs along with communication and support units. Many firefighters—indeed, many entire units—were not on duty but took it upon themselves to suit up and get to ground zero.

The rescue and containment effort was underway. Things were still in disarray, and most everyone—police, firefighters, and EMTs—still looked at the scene with a sort of shocked disbelief. But on this day, New York's Finest—a term usually reserved for the police department but, I believe, applicable to all who served for the good of all at that moment in history—were there just doing what they do. And in doing so, they saved lives.

For fifty-six harrowing minutes, this continued on. Some people were able to escape the burning buildings; hundreds of others who saw no way out began to jump or perhaps fall from the Twin Towers' upper floors. Many who had been working above the floors where the planes had impacted the buildings did not even know what exactly was happening, but the views from their gutted offices could not have given them too much hope.

The South Tower, miraculously, had one undamaged stairwell that allowed many people to leave their workplaces and head for safety. But in the North Tower, the plane's impact had obliterated all stairwells, which ran down the center of the building, leaving no escape route for the more than 1,300 people left stranded on the floors above. Some headed for the roof, hoping for rescue by helicopter from there. But the roof access doors were locked, and with the thick smoke the burning towers were emitting, no helicopter would have been able to approach anyway.

Not many who were on the topmost floors of the buildings when the planes hit were able to make it out alive. In the South Tower, whether they had access to that one stairwell or were trapped up above, their fate became the same in that fifty-sixth minute after the second plane struck, as the building collapsed on itself and was demolished right down to the ground. It took another thirty-two minutes for the North Tower to follow suit at 10:28 a.m. Weakened not just by the impacts but by the fires it caused and the explosions ignited by the planes' fuel, the buildings' structures had simply given out. They were just shy of thirty years old and were global icons of international business and the American corporate world. And now, in just under an hour, they were no more.

In the immediate aftermath of the destruction of the World Trade Center towers, no one knew what to do. Those who were thankfully out of harm's way but saw the entire thing happen either stared in mute horror or screamed and cried until their voices and their tears gave out. Those closest to and at the site of the collapsed buildings—which was, from that moment onward, referred to as Ground Zero—were stunned, injured, and in shock but fortunate, for the time being, to have made it out alive.

Even if they hadn't been inside one of the buildings or directly outside them when they came down, if they were near enough, they were likely trapped within the massive clouds of dust created by the falling towers. As each building went down, a plume of pulverized construction materials and debris shot high up into the air and then fell at rapid speed, creating a zone of negative air pressure that forced the clouds to roll out down the canyons of the city's streets, burying everything and everyone it encountered, even breaking windows and rushing inside nearby homes and shops. Those who were trapped within the cloud described it as being pitch black, so thick that it did not even let through the sunshine that had been so abundant on that clear, beautiful morning.

When the cloud finally dissipated enough for people to see and move around, they found all of Lower Manhattan covered in a thick coat of the stuff; it looked as if there had been a very heavy snowfall, though the precipitation was a dank gray instead of a bright white. The dust consisted, we now know, of thousands of tons of toxic debris and more than 2,500 contaminants including asbestos, lead, mercury, and various carcinogens; this made 9/11 not only the worst terrorist attack on American soil but one of the worst environmental disasters we have suffered as well.

In the thirteen years since the attacks, many studies have shown the detrimental effects that exposure to the dust likely had on the health not just of the responders and the people caught within the cloud but of people who lived in nearby neighborhoods. Up to sixty-five thousand people, some estimates say, who had direct or indirect contact with the dust have suffered or have the potential to be stricken with everything from impaired lung function to pregnancy issues such as prematurity and low birthweight to an excessively increased risk of various cancers including melanoma, lymphoma, leukemia, and cancers of the lungs, kidneys, bladder, colon, and breasts. In fact since 2001, more than 1,100 first responders and people who worked or lived in Lower Manhattan have been diagnosed.

Some estimates also say that up to 422,000 New Yorkers have suffered or currently suffer from post-traumatic stress disorder due to the attacks. In the direct aftermath, more than a million of us would change any air travel plans we had, opting to go by train or car instead. More than twenty thousand apartments (the main form of habitation in New York City) in Lower Manhattan were eligible for asbestos cleanup, and another twenty thousand requested the service on top of that. Twenty percent of all Americans knew someone who had been hurt or killed, and more than three thousand children lost at least one parent.

A total of 291 intact bodies were recovered from the

World Trade Center site along with 21,744 quantities labeled as "remains." The number of families who received no bodies or remains was 1,717.

However, at the moment, that was all in the future—another event that no one could have seen coming. Directly after the 9/11 attacks, it did not take long for the rescue phase of the operation to begin. As soon as visibility increased enough, the first responders who remained headed back to where the buildings had once stood, to see if there were any survivors. Some were found among the rubble—severely injured, mostly, yet still alive. However, those were few and far between. The majority of people who had been in or near the Twin Towers when they collapsed did not make it out alive, and the situation quickly turned into a recovery effort instead.

In the following days, weeks, and months, the death toll climbed and climbed as ongoing searches through seas of rubble and debris not only at the World Trade Center but also at the Pentagon and in Shanksville turned up many bodies (or, more accurately, body parts) but few survivors. In total, 2,977 innocent people were killed, including 405 of the brave souls of the NYPD and FDNY and the EMTs who were caught in or around the collapsing buildings. Seventeen entire firefighting units were wiped out in a fell swoop. One hundred and twenty-eight companies and organizations who occupied offices in either of the World Trade Center's Twin Towers lost much or most of their staff; the most widely known is Cantor Fitzgerald, an investment bank that occupied the 101st to 105th floors of One World Trade Center; they lost 658 of their 960 employees.

Since the attacks, an estimated 19,000 people have become sick or even died due to illnesses or effects believed to be related to the September 11 attack on the World Trade Center, including more than 1,400 rescue workers who gave up their time, and ultimately their lives, to look for survivors, retrieve the dead, and restore a sense of safety to New York City.

Though the majority of those who perished at the World Trade Center were US citizens, there were individuals representing more than 115 countries who lost their lives as well. The average age of those who died was forty years old, though there were five children, from ages three to eleven, on the two airplanes, and even eleven known unborn babies who were also taken.

None of these figures, however, include the nineteen hijackers—all members of al-Qaeda—who carried out the attacks.

Six

The previous chapter presented the facts—the things we all learned during and after the September 11 attacks thanks to extensive research and investigation by various law enforcement, governmental, and military agencies. This is what we saw on the news or read in newspapers or online, the details that we discussed with friends and colleagues and over dinner with our families at night. And we believed them because, quite simply, they were true. Looking at the facts, it wasn't difficult to see the story that had happened here: Al-Qaeda hates the United States, al-Qaeda came up with a way to strike fear into America's heart, al-Qaeda carried out that plan, and this was where we ended up.

If it's not quite obvious enough, I'll state it again: Al-Qaeda was to blame. They even took credit for it in a series of video, audio, and printed statements and interviews—this came from senior members of the organization, too, so the admissions were viewed as credible. And it took our FBI only two weeks after the attacks to trace the hijackers to al-Qaeda. So we had proof from both sides.

Yet, there are some people—US citizens, no less, people who enjoy all the freedoms our military has fought for and won for us and that our government ensures will remain intact—who question the truth of these explanations. They believe in all the conspiracy theories they read on the Internet: that the collapse of the Twin Towers (and, later, neighboring 7 World Trade Center, on which part of the fuselage from one of the planes had landed) was due to a controlled demolition; that a missile hit the Pentagon, not a plane; that our own government orchestrated the attacks to create an excuse to invade Afghanistan and Iraq. And there are dozens more, each more absurd than the last.

Why do people believe these things? Why do they take the lies for truth? I imagine it makes them feel powerful—that they "know" something most people don't, which makes them, in their eyes, smarter. They see the US government as the guilty party, which, so they think, makes them more enlightened than the average person because they do not blindly trust, as they think everyone else does.

Now, I am all for critical thinking. And if the government does something wrong, yes, hold it accountable. This is why we have courts, oversight committees, and checks and balances. But I can say with absolute certainty that in this case, the government did nothing wrong. There was no secret plot to kill almost three thousand of our own people; what would the government get out of that?

Still the conspiracies persist. And in the interest of quelling and disproving them, I'd like to discuss some of them here.

Demolition

Many people have raised the idea that the destruction of the World Trade Center towers was the result of a controlled demolition. This means that some entity—a company specializing in razing buildings, for example, or even the military or governmental agents, according to some—went into the towers before the planes hit them and rigged them with enough explosives to make them crumble to the ground. This theory was first floated to the public just a month after the attacks and continues to survive through today thanks to several books published on the subject (or on 9/11 conspiracies in general, including this one), many websites, and general word of mouth.

Conspiracy theorists who have set their sights on this idea use several points to back up their claims, including the following:

The ways in which the buildings fell. Since the planes hit the towers at high floors, one would have expected, theorists say, for the tops of the buildings to detach and topple over. The fact that both buildings seemed to fall nearly straight down is suspect to many who believe this conspiracy. To them, the destruction was far too tidy, with the buildings falling in on themselves in a very orderly fashion, just as would happen with any controlled demolition carried out with explosives.

The speed at which the buildings fell. Some have referred to the ways in which the towers fell as a sort of free fall, meaning they were able to pick up velocity as they continued down with nothing impeding them. The official theory is that the buildings fell pancake-style—that is, each floor collapsing onto the one below it in a chain reaction down to the bottom. If this were so, say the conspiracy theorists, each successive floor would have caused more resistance, slowing down the total destruction time. Instead, the collapses seemed almost instantaneous.

The temperature of melting steel. This is one of the most debated topics in all of the 9/11 conspiracies. According to the official analysis of what happened to the World Trade Center on that day, the cores of the towers—each formed by forty-seven separate and massive steel columns—were damaged by the impacts of the airplanes and then further compromised by the fires resulting from the crashes, particularly the burning of the jet fuel. After 56 and 102 minutes, the cores of the South and North Towers, respectively, could no longer hold due to this damage, and the collapses ensued.

According to the conspiracy theorists, however, it would have taken much more than a "simple" jet-fuel fire to melt those thick, nearly indestructible steel columns. That they melted at least in part is not the issue being argued. People working in the rubble of the buildings reported seeing molten steel among the wreckage, and there are indeed photographs of it. Also, there were reports of liquefied metal pouring out of the South Tower prior to its demise. These both point to the fact that yes, there was structural breakdown of the buildings' cores due to extremely elevated temperatures.

The issue, then, is *how* elevated those temperatures were. Conspiracy theorists have an often-repeated mantra that it would take much more heat than a building and/or airplane fire could produce to melt steel of that gauge far enough that it would cause an entire skyscraper to collapse. This, they say, points to there having been explosives in or around the beams, placed there specifically to melt the steel.

The total destruction of the towers. That the World Trade Center's main buildings were essentially pulverized as they fell shows, to some people, that there were definitely additional explosives involved in their demolition. It's true, there was little left one could identify as a piece of a building after all was said and done; what remained were bits and pieces of walls and windows and scraps of metal that once constituted the buildings' frames. Considering this, conspiracy theorists say that it would be unusual for there to be no significant portions left of a building that underwent a structural collapse due to failure of its parts. Further, they believe, an accidental collapse—in contrast to a controlled demolition—would not generate enough gravitational force to destroy the materials of the buildings so completely.

Why This Conspiracy Theory Doesn't Work

One idea I always go back to when thinking about this conspiracy theory is that nothing like the September 11 terrorists attacks had ever happened to our country. So can we really say we could predict how any of it was supposed to happen? Yes, the iron cores of the World Trade Center buildings were strong; they had been constructed to withstand heavy winds, fires, and even earthquakes though they're rarely experienced in New York. But who ever could have thought that two airplanes would fly into them? None of us did, not even those of us who were on the front lines of the ongoing war on terror. And so the architects who had designed the buildings back in the 1970s did not do so with that in mind.

Given this, I find it difficult to hear people say that each building should have behaved a certain way as it withstood the impact of an 877,000-pound airplane, was engulfed in raging fire from the burning jet fuel, and then collapsed. This was an entirely new and inexplicably horrifying experience for us. There was nothing we had to compare it to in order to gauge if the speed and uniformity of the collapse were typical or not.

Next let's look at the conspiracy theorists' assertion that in order to melt the buildings' steel cores, there would have had to be an additional and hotter heat source on top of the jet fuel fires. This one is very simple to disprove. Typically, steel in its most generally used form can withstand heat up to almost 1,300 degrees Fahrenheit. The fuel used in the planes that crashed into the buildings has a maximum burning temperature of 1,796 degrees Fahrenheit. The math doesn't seem to be ambiguous here.

We Knew

Probably the most well-known—and, sadly, most widely believed—conspiracy theory regarding the September 11 terrorist attacks has to do with the US government's foreknowledge of the events, or the belief that we—the US government, military, and other factions—knew that the attacks were going to happen and in fact allowed them to happen to further our own agendas. Those who buy in to this theory believe, among other things:

Wall Street Knew. There was some unusual stock market activity prior to the 9/11 attacks. United Airlines and American Airlines—the two involved in all four plane crashes on that day—saw abnormally high put options just prior to the attacks. (A put option allows the holder of the option to sell the asset at a specified price by a predetermined time.) This was also true for insurance companies such as Citigroup, whose Travelers Insurance later paid out more than $500 million in claims relating to the World Trade Center attack. In contrast, on September 10 the call options—which allow the holder to buy the stock at a certain price—increased dramatically for defense contractor Raytheon.

Our air defense was told to stand down. Conspiracy theorists believe that after the first plane involved in the terrorist attacks the North American Aerospace Defense Command (NORAD) could have and should have sent out fighters to locate and take down any other airplanes that were involved before they reached their targets. NORAD had this capability and the power to exercise it, but they did not send out any fighter jets until everything was said and done. The only explanation for this, the theorists believe, is that NORAD had been told not to dispatch any fighter jets or issue any response to the alerts that were coming in about the attacks.

Why This Conspiracy Theory Doesn't Work

This one can be difficult to disprove with hard facts and figures, because how can you ever verify for sure what someone did or did not know? Still, I find this set of theories indefensible, mostly because I work for the US government as a member of its standing military, and I have full faith that our government would never do anything like what I described above. That the leaders of our nation would willingly and on purpose kill its own citizens and cause billions of dollars' worth of property damage, not to mention the psychological trauma we all underwent just from witnessing it and the ongoing illnesses the 9/11 first responders and others still suffer from the event—it just doesn't make sense to me. There is no agenda on Earth that I can think of that would justify such means, and while I know there are some government operations that are not public knowledge simply for security reasons, I do not believe those in charge of running our country would be so evil as to undertake a covert mission that would end in the loss of thousands of lives, something that would change our way of life forever.

Some conspiracy theorists truly seem to believe that this is true, though—that the US government planned the events of September 11, 2001, or at least allowed them to happen, in order to have an excuse to invade the countries of Iraq and Afghanistan. To that, I say: If we had wanted to invade those nations, we had very good reasons to before 9/11 and did not need any further "excuse" to do so. In Iraq, Saddam Hussein was harboring weapons of mass destruction; in Afghanistan, the Taliban, an Islamic fundamentalist political group which harbored terrorist groups including al-Qaeda, massacred Afghan civilians and literally burned vast areas of the country right down to the ground. These were cause enough, in my opinion, for us to send our troops into these countries.

No Plane Hit the Pentagon

In a truly stunning assertion, some conspiracy theorists have claimed that it was not a passenger plane that plowed into the side of the Pentagon on the morning of September 11, 2001; instead, they say, it was a missile and that our government authorized and even planned to use. Most who believe this looked at the hole the crash left in the Pentagon building and decided it was too small to have been made by a commercial plane; they also say the security camera footage, which we discussed earlier, showed a much smaller craft—if any at all. Had a passenger jet truly hit the building, theorists believe, it would have shown up on the footage simply due to its enormous size.

Why This Conspiracy Theory Doesn't Work

It is true that it's difficult to see in the security footage what exactly is flying into the Pentagon just prior to the explosion that ripped the building apart. However, consider this: A plane's maximum speed can reach up to 570 miles per hour. Given their intention, the hijackers flying this plane most likely did not slow down very much as they brought the plane down toward the ground, meaning perhaps it picked up even more velocity with the pull of gravity. Now consider that the average security camera, such as the one that recorded the attack on the Pentagon, does not run continuously but takes single snapshots at intervals such as five seconds or ten seconds. Even if this camera had been set at ten or more, imagine how far an 800,000-pound aircraft traveling at the speed mentioned above could go in ten seconds. Or five. Or three. At that rate, it could become nearly invisible to a stop-motion camera.

The theory that the hole left in the Pentagon from the plane's crash was not large enough has been debunked by a professor of civil engineering at Purdue University who noted that one of American Airlines flight 77's wings had hit the ground just prior to its impact with the Pentagon, and the other wing was demolished as it struck the building's load-bearing columns. This would leave the fuselage, with a narrower width, to create the hole in question. Additionally, *Architecture Week* magazine asserted that the affected area of the Pentagon building had just been renovated, which meant the edifice was made of newer and thus more durable materials.

Last is the conspiracy theorists' assertion that a missile, not a plane, hit the Pentagon. There is much evidence to contradict this. First, there were eyewitnesses who saw the plane crashing into the building. Second, the passengers on the plane had placed phone calls while onboard to report the hijacking (though of course the theorists believe these were also faked). Third, a massive amount of airplane debris was recovered at the site, from landing gear to a cockpit seat to the all-important black boxes. Last, the remains of many passengers from the flight were also found on the scene. How much more evidence do they need than that?

Flight 93 Was Shot Down

This conspiracy theory posits that United flight 93, which crashed outside of Shanksville, Pennsylvania, was actually shot down by a US fighter jet—one of the late starters, we can assume, issued by NORAD once they got around to it, as conspiracy theorists believe. The evidence, the theorists say, is that debris and large parts of the plane, including an engine, landed eight miles from the main crash site, which is unusual for a "normal" airline disaster. Some also say there is proof that damage to the engine had been caused by a heat-seeking missile. Others believe the decimated nature of the plane's remains show it must have been demolished in some highly unusual and extraordinary way.

Still others go to even further extremes, asserting that United flight 93 didn't crash at all but was simply rerouted to a secret location, and another plane went in to take its place in the crash. Its passengers allegedly now live in hiding, but are safe. In another theory, the plane landed but all onboard were murdered, presumably to silence them. To theorists, it's entirely plausible that the people on the plane had found out about the government's plot to let 9/11 happen, so they had to be taken out.

Why This Conspiracy Theory Doesn't Work

First, there are logistic inaccuracies. The engine of the plane did not land miles away but a mere three hundred yards and in an area that was consistent with the direction of the plane's travel. Some debris was recovered up to eight miles away, but this was things such as papers that passengers had been transporting and pieces of the plane's insulation, all of which could have been carried by the wind. Besides, the area where they were found, Indian Lake, was only a mile from the crash site as the crow flies; the road to get there was nearly seven miles, but obviously this plane did not take that road. Thus, the distance was not even correct.

Some conspiracy theorists have claimed that eyewitnesses saw a small, white plane flying above where United flight 93 crashed, and that this plane had fired the missile that had brought down the passenger jet. In fact, there was a small craft in the area, but it was a Dassault Falcon business jet that had been asked by local air traffic control to descend from a higher elevation and survey the wreckage. There were no military aircraft in the vicinity of flight 93.

Last, the idea that the crash had been fabricated and the passengers forced into hiding needs no refutation. There is evidence that people from the plane called authorities and loved ones to report what was happening. The passengers' attempted takeover during the hijacking was captured on the cockpit recorder. Large and small parts of the plane were recovered on the ground, as were passengers' remains and their effects. There is no need to go into detail in disproving this farce.

The Hijackings Were Faked

Shortly after the terrorist attacks on September 11, 2001, the British Broadcasting Company (BBC) published a partial list of people believed to be the plane hijackers who carried out the terrorist acts. While most of the names on the list were accurately tied to the hijackers who had died in the attacks, several were found to be linked to people who were still alive, leading some in the general public to believe that the hijackings were faked—that because some of the terrorists were potentially alive, none of the ones who died could have existed.

Why This Conspiracy Theory Doesn't Work
It's no secret that in the days and weeks after the September 11 attacks, our nation and indeed the world devolved at times into chaos. In trying to figure out what had really happened and who we could say was responsible for it, while at the same time dealing with the aftermath of this monumental and ultimately jarring tragedy, we followed many leads and sometimes, as happens, hit dead ends. Unfortunately, this meant that misinformation was released to the public on occasions, as happened with the BBC.

The fact was that some of the names they published were

just plain wrong—or, rather, they were the correct names but referring to different people. It's not difficult to believe there could be more than one John Smith or Jane Brown in the world, and these names were like that. Our own FBI sorted out the mess and revealed the cases of mistaken identity.

Still, people continue to make this leap not just of faith but of logic and reality, and the theory, unfortunately, still persists.

Foreign Governments Were Involved

This conspiracy claims that several nations around the world had knowledge of the 9/11 terrorist plot or contributed to it in some way. Some say either Pakistan or Saudi Arabia or both provided funds to make the attacks happen; a Lloyds of London insurance company actually sued the latter for repayment of the £136 million it paid to victims of the attacks.

Some believe Israel, in particular Mossad (its national intelligence agency), had the all-important foreknowledge that the attacks were imminent. Both a former head of Pakistan's Inter-Services Intelligence agency and a former president of Italy, for example, claimed the attacks had been carried out by the CIA and Mossad working in conjunction.

In fact, Israel has borne the brunt of many conspiracy theorists' ire. Some say Israel's government, Mossad, or prime minister at the time, Ariel Sharon, planned the attacks and carried them out to divert attention from Israel's conflict with Palestine; to induce the United States to attack their enemies, particularly some notoriously anti-Semitic Middle Eastern countries; or to put Zionists in a position to control world affairs. Their evidence: a rumor that nearly four thousand Jewish employees who worked at the World Trade Center were told ahead of time to stay home on September 11.

Why This Conspiracy Theory Doesn't Work
While it is true that fewer Jews died in the 9/11 attacks than did followers of any other religion—estimated between 270 and 400 in the World Trade Center towers alone—there are perfectly reasonable explanations for this. First, these numbers are well in line with the percentage of Jewish people living in New York at the time. Second, these numbers are based on only *partial* surveys of victims' religions, meaning the sampling could have been small and the actual deaths much higher. In addition, five Israeli citizens perished in the attacks; if this conspiracy theory were valid, wouldn't they have been warned too?

There Were No Planes

Perhaps one of the most offensive conspiracy theories asserts that no planes flew into the World Trade Center buildings—that it would have been impossible for a commercial airliner to penetrate the towers' steel hulls, and all of the photographs and video footage we have of them doing so has been faked. This is, obviously, an enormous claim to make; if there were no planes, then what really happened to the Twin Towers?

Overall, these theorists agree that two missiles, not planes, hit the buildings, but of course that was not what we have been led to believe. This is not what the pictures and videos in the media have shown us all along. And that is because, according to the theorists, those images have been one of two things:

Digital composites. This means that several pictures were laid one on top of the other to create a single image. So images of airplanes flying toward the buildings could have been superimposed on top of images of the World Trade Center burning—after being hit by the alleged missiles.

Holograms. It's also been said that the images we see are actually of the missiles striking the towers, but they are surrounded by airplane-shaped holograms, so we can't tell the difference. Frighteningly, this theory came from a former chief economist in the US Labor Department.

Why This Conspiracy Theory Doesn't Work

There has been no evidence of missiles having struck the towers but plenty showing that two airplanes did, from pieces of the landing gear lying in the street to an engine landing on the 7 World Trade Center building.

More important, though, is that pictures don't lie. Fabricating and re-creating the probably millions of photographs and thousands of videos made of the events of that day in New York would be an impossible task. Whoever could be in charge of this would have had to collect all evidence not just from the media outlets around the world that took or showed footage and images but from every single photograph and videographer who had been there in person and recorded what happened. This includes people in both New York and New Jersey; there were even pictures taken by satellites orbiting the Earth and by an International Space Station expedition team.

Collecting all these—particularly those last ones—would be truly more than one lifetime's work.

Plus, there were eyewitnesses who saw the planes impacting the buildings. If it were one or two people, sure, one could make a case that they were lying. But thousands? Millions? What about the people who were trapped in the buildings and made it out alive—the ones who saw the plane hit the *other* building? Or those simply walking by on the street who were killed by falling airplane pieces or scalded with burning jet fuel raining down from the sky?

It just would not be possible to fake any part of an event of this magnitude—something as enormous, horrifying and messy as the 9/11 terrorist attacks turned out to be.

The Cover-Ups

Cover-ups are the meat and potatoes, as it were, of conspiracy theorists, so it's no surprise how many have been alleged regarding the September 11 attacks. All the conspiracy theories discussed above are dependent upon a belief in cover-ups in order to work; to believe them, you must believe that there is a layer of so-called truth to which most common people are not privy.

On a certain level, this is true: Our government and military do keep some information highly classified, but that is mostly to control the level of security that is necessary to keep the participants in the operations out of harm's way. It is not because the government has nefarious plans, nor does it wish to manipulate the lives of its own citizens. There are those who believe such things—that the government is an evil entity bent only on amassing power both within and outside of our borders—but I just can't see how it could be. Would such a corrupt government offer financial assistance to its poorest citizens? Would it broker peace talks between warring nations, aid to third world countries, and pledges of military assistance wherever it is needed? Our government is altruistic, not immoral. It is protective, not coercive. And just because we might not know every single move it makes, that doesn't mean it is keeping secrets from us.

Unfortunately, not everyone agrees. For example, some see cover-ups in the following subjects:

Recovery of the black boxes. The 9/11 Commission Report—the official, government-ordered, independent investigation into and analysis of the terrorist attacks of September 11, 2001—stated that no black boxes were recovered in the World Trade Center rubble from either of the airplanes involved in the attacks that day (every plane usually has two of them).

A black box, also known as a cockpit voice recorder or a flight data recorder, captures audio within the cockpit of a plane through the pilots' earpieces and microphones as well as through a microphone mounted in the ceiling. When there is an airplane crash, investigators always want to find the black box (so named for the nearly indestructible box in which the recorder is contained—which, ironically, is bright orange) in order to hear what went on in the front of the plane prior to the incident, hoping the recording will give some clue to what went wrong.

So you can see why finding these planes' black boxes would

be so important: They might have given us some clues as to how the planes were overtaken, what the hijackers' motives were, and so on. The 9/11 Commission Report noted that both black boxes from American Airlines Flight 77, which crashed into the Pentagon, and United flight 93, which crashed in Pennsylvania, were recovered though the recorder from the former was too damaged to provide any data. (Remember, they are *nearly* indestructible.)

At the World Trade Center, though? Nothing turned up—at least not officially. According to the conspiracy theorists, however, two men who worked on the cleanup of the World Trade Center site did find and remove three of the four black boxes from flights 11 and 75, and they did so with the full knowledge and in fact under the orders of the FBI.

Osama bin Laden's confessions. As the founder of the al-Qaeda terrorist network, bin Laden released several audio and video tapes of himself in the years after the 9/11 attacks, and in them he took responsibility for the attacks—except for in the first one, where he completely denied it. However, the US government's translation was inaccurate in order to cover this up.

Known as the Jalalabad tape, this video recording was released in December 2001. There have been questions as to its authenticity and whether or not bin Laden is really the featured speaker; some in the 9/11 Truth organization have contested that the facial features and weight of the man in the video differ from bin Laden's and that he is shown writing with his right hand although bin Laden is left handed.

However, the CIA concluded it was truly him, and our government's translators did their best to decipher what he was trying to say. What it amounted to was an admission that he had been the mastermind behind the September 11 terrorist attacks. Conspiracy theorists, however, believe that his words were misinterpreted—possibly on purpose—and that his message was really that he took no responsibility, that whomever this man was, he'd had nothing to do with the attacks. (For more about bin Laden, see chapter seven.)

The CIA recruiting known terrorists. Conspiracy theorists have asserted that the CIA, prior to September 2001, had been trying to recruit Nawaf al-Hazmi and Khalid al-Mihdhar—two known terrorists and, later, two of the hijackers who flew the planes into the Pentagon on September 11, presumably to use as moles or double agents—people on the inside of the Muslim extremist movement who could witness what was going on and report back to the US government. In so doing, it is said, the CIA withheld information about the two men from other government agencies, including those that might have been able to track the men's movements and whereabouts prior to the terrorist attacks—and, it is surmised, possibly uncover the plot and bring it to a halt.

Why This Conspiracy Theory Doesn't Work

On April 18, 2012, the families of those who died on United flight 93, the plane that crashed in Pennsylvania, were given the opportunity by the FBI to listen to the contents of the cockpit voice recorder from that plane if they chose. If black boxes from the other planes had been recovered, the same would have been done with them, so we can assume that no black boxes were found.

As far as bin Laden's claims or the lack thereof, in November

2007 he released an audiotape in which he did undeniably claim responsibility for the attacks. Two other major planners of the plot also confessed as to their involvement during interviews at other times. Is it possible that the man in the first recording was not bin Laden? Or that it was bin Laden and he claimed that he did not orchestrate the attacks? Yes, both are within the realm of possibility. But the fact of the matter is, bin Laden or not, admission or not, the real bin Laden did go on to say that he and al-Qaeda had planned and carried out the terrorist attacks on the United States that took place on September 11, 2001. What more evidence could one need than that?

And, as I have noted before, it is no secret that, yes, our government sometimes has to keep secrets from us. This is not out of any form of malice but an abundance of caution for those involved in what can sometimes be incredibly sensitive operations—ones in which their or others' lives are at stake. This includes military personnel and individuals and teams from government agencies such as the CIA and the FBI. So it comes as no surprise to me that if the CIA had any connection to Nawaf al-Hazmi and Khalid al-Mihdhar—and that is a very, very big *if*—they kept it under wraps. Who knows what kinds of ties the two men had or what kind of chain reaction the CIA's investigation could have caused had it been made public knowledge?

The list here could go on and on. Conspiracy theories about 9/11 are almost as numerous as the victims who lost their lives that day. Who believes them? There are several organized groups, including Architects & Engineers for 9/11 Truth, 9/11 Truth, Scholars for 9/11 Truth, and 9/11 Citizens Watch among many, many others. Some of these groups maintain active websites for discussion of September 11 conspiracy theories and discoveries; some have written and published books on the subject.

No matter their method, however, it's clear that what they're promoting is dangerous, libelous, and ultimately harmful information. If we look at any subject or event closely enough, we can find aspects of it that don't quite seem to fit together in our minds; that doesn't mean such theories are always true. (Hence the word *theory*, which means "an idea that is suggested or presented as possibly true but that is not known or proven to be true.") Often it's merely a case of seeing what we want to see. Those who distrust the government to begin with want to find reasons in the September 11 attacks to prove their distrust; those who are anti-Muslim or anti-Israel or even anti-American will find their reasons too because in an event this big, such a monumental catastrophe, there are so many nooks and crevices, it can be very easy to get stuck on a small, seemingly anomalous fact. It is only when we can pull back and look at the big picture that we see how that piece fits into the whole. This, it seems, is a capacity that conspiracy theorists do not possess.

Seven

In September 2001, every American—and indeed people around the world—became aware of who Osama bin Laden was and that he was the head of a terrorist network called al-Qaeda. Within only two weeks of the 9/11 attacks, our FBI had tracked the airplane hijackers back to al-Qaeda, the group that trained them, sponsored them, and planned the atrocities they carried out.

But this does not mean that al-Qaeda simply sprung into being right before that month. In fact, the group has been around since 1988 or 1989, when Osama bin Laden, along with Abdullah Azzam and several others, founded it as a multinational, baseless military force, of sorts—a network, as I have called it, of individuals and "cells" throughout the world that could be activated and trained at will to carry out what the group saw as a global jihad, or, as it is interpreted, the Muslim struggle against those who do not believe in Allah, the Islamic god. *Jihad* is also often used to mean some sort of holy war, and that indeed is exactly what bin Laden and his followers have been waging against the Western world, particularly the United States. Their alleged reasons for this are many, and we will examine them below. But first, let's take a look inside al-Qaeda and what brought the group to carry out the September 11 terrorist attacks.

Inside al-Qaeda

Though I mentioned above that bin Laden and his cohorts formed al-Qaeda in the late 1980s, in truth its origins go back another decade, to the Soviet War in Afghanistan, which started in 1979. This conflict pitted the Soviets and Afghan Marxists against the Afghan mujahideen, or the radical Muslim militants who carried out the jihad in the first sense mentioned above: as the struggle against those who did not follow Allah or what they believed to be Allah's way; in this case, the Afghan Marxist regime. Believing this was nothing but an opportunistic grab for land expansion on the part of the Soviet Union, the United States threw its considerable weight behind the small mujahideen force of only about 250,000, funneling hundreds of millions of dollars to the cause throughout the war via the Pakistani Inter-Services Intelligence agency.

The mujahideen also received considerable support from the Arab community, many of whom joined the jihad; others supported them through monetary donations. In all, Arab organizations, including some funded by the Saudi Arabian government and Saudi businessmen, donated more than $600 million a year to the jihad. Much of these funds came as direct results of bin Laden's solicitation of them from wealthy individuals and organizations.

When the Soviet Union withdrew from Afghanistan in 1989, so did US aid to the mujahideen, but the struggle was not over. At that point, the communist government in the country stayed in power for a few more years before the mujahideen finally took over, but they did not have a coherent structure and goals, and so the leadership of Afghanistan devolved into chaos. It was then that some mujahideen turned their sights on the Islamic struggle in other countries, and toward that end several smaller offshoot groups were formed.

One of them was al-Qaeda, which held its first meeting on August 11, 1988, though it did not use its official name in public at the time because its existence was considered top secret. There was tumult from the outset as the group's two main leaders, bin Laden and Azzam, could not agree on whether or not to militarize their operations; the former voted no, the latter voted yes. The conflict was resolved a year later when Azzam was assassinated and al-Qaeda split into factions. Most adherents at that time chose to follow bin Laden.

How, then, did the one who chose the side of peace end up as the head of one of the most violent terrorist factions in existence? It started during the First Gulf War, when the United States sent troops to the Middle East to help Kuwait defend itself against invading Iraqi forces who sought to control the country. In the process, Saudi Arabia found itself in danger as well, as its oil fields were within shooting distance from the occupying Iraqi military in Kuwait. Seeing the problem, and having already had much experience with war, bin Laden went to King Fahd of Saudi Arabia and offered the services of his group of mujahideen. However, the king declined and chose instead to allow US forces to enter Saudi territory to help defend it—a very controversial decision, as Saudi Arabia is considered the birthplace of Islam and the most holy land of that religion. It is the home of Mecca, toward which all Muslims pray on a daily basis, and every year millions of Muslims make pilgrimages there to profess, express, and reinforce their faith.

This angered bin Laden—that non-Muslims would be allowed on such sacred soil when his soldiers could do the job just as well, if not better because they had the will of Allah to guide them. And he expressed his anger to the king. In response, Fahd banished bin Laden from his beloved Saudi Arabia, his homeland, forcing him to live in exile. Bin Laden's enmity was further increased in 1993, when the Saudi king supported the Oslo Accords, the goal of which was peace between Israel and Palestine, and then again the following year, when King Fahd revoked bin Laden's Saudi citizenship for his continued and very vocal disapproval of the king.

To top it all off, bin Laden's very wealthy family cut off his $7 million a month allowance, and any assets he had in Saudi Arabia were frozen. He now was poor, he was exiled from his homeland, and he was estranged from his family. He had nothing and no one left but his anger and his group of militants, al-Qaeda. And it all had begun with the United States sending military aid to Saudi Arabia. So obviously it was our fault.

When he was banished from Saudi Arabia, bin Laden received an invitation to base al-Qaeda out of Sudan, and he accepted that offer. Using this nation as their new headquarters, al-Qaeda set up camps to train its soldiers—until 1996, when bin Laden was exiled from Sudan as well for his involvement in a failed assassination attempt on Egyptian president Hosni Mubarak. At that point, he returned to Afghanistan, where the fledgling Taliban, an Islamic fundamentalist group, had taken over the government and was working to institute a strict interpretation of sharia law. Bin Laden found a home there; he joined the new government's Ministry of Defense, and the Taliban put him in charge of training an elite mujahideen faction of their army, many of whom had fought in the Soviet-Afghanistan war.

This too ended for bin Laden when, in 2001, the United

States' Operation Enduring Freedom brought down the Taliban government and captured or killed many of the elite brigade's soldiers.

Those who survived went to Pakistan with bin Laden—or so it was believed. From that point on, the man was like a ghost, appearing here and there but then always seeming to be gone when we went to look for him. From wherever his hiding spots were, however, he was able to keep al-Qaeda running and in fact increase its numbers by reaching out to mujahideen worldwide, to those Muslims who wished to carry out a global jihad: to rid Muslim lands of all non-Muslims through the most brutal methods, with a very high body count. In doing so, bin Laden initiated what can be seen as an offensive (rather than defensive) period of the global jihad.

The Campaigns

The first thing bin Laden sought to do through al-Qaeda was to rid all Islamic lands of foreign military presences. Toward this end, he issued a *fatwa*—a statement issued by an Islamic scholar (bin Laden, assumedly, was self-appointed) that carries great weight and is based on religious scripture—calling on all followers of the Islamic faith to kill all Americans they see as well as any American allies. The focus of al-Qaeda thus shifted from national or regional to large-scale military-esque operations.

Yemen
The new al-Qaeda's first public show of force came in December 1992, when they detonated bombs outside two hotels in Yemen

in attempts to kill US soldiers en route to providing famine relief in Somalia. No American lives were taken as the hotel where they were staying was not one of the two targeted, but still al-Qaeda declared this a victory because it did in fact cause the Americans to leave the area out of preemptive caution.

New York
The following year, al-Qaeda made another unsuccessful strike, this time in New York, and a bit more indirectly. Ramzi Yousef, who had attended at terrorist training camp in Afghanistan, parked a truck bomb in the underground garage of the World Trade Center. The explosive device did detonate, but it did not accomplish all Yousef intended. His aim was to damage the foundation of Tower One so it would fall over, knocking over Tower Two in the process and, he hoped, killing a couple hundred thousand people. Instead, the towers shook a little, but the foundation remained intact, and, unfortunately, six people died.

Yousef later went on to develop plans to blow up American airplanes, to assassinate the pope and US President Clinton, and to crash a plane into CIA headquarters. None of these came to fruition, and he was later captured in Pakistan. (Bin Laden himself later plotted to kill Clinton as well, but the CIA intercepted a communication that helped them to prevent it.)

East Africa
In August 7, 1998—the eighth anniversary of the US military forces' arrival in Saudi Arabia to protect it against Iraq—al-Qaeda put themselves on the international map by carrying out a series of simultaneous bombings at US embassies in Dar es Salaam and Nairobi, killing more than three hundred people.

Although bin Laden was not the mastermind of this plot—that title went to two of his cohorts, Fazul Abdullah Mohammed and Abdullah Ahmed Abdullah—following this incident, the FBI put bin Laden on its ten most-wanted fugitives list as he had made dozens of calls to his associates regarding the bombings. In response to these attacks, the US military launched cruise missiles at an al-Qaeda base in Afghanistan, leaving it decimated.

The Millennium Bombings

Fortunately, this was a campaign that never made it off the ground. Prior to the end of the twentieth century, al-Qaeda planned another series of bombings to take place in late 1999 and early 2000 to coincide with the turn of the millennium—undoubtedly a time of great celebration for many people worldwide. They planned to bomb Christian holy sites, airports, and a US destroyer. Watching for signs of these attacks and patrolling off the coast of New York City were among my duties while part of the Navy's IBU-24 (see chapter four for more on this).

Yemen

As we looked at earlier, in October 2000 al-Qaeda did succeed in bombing a US military ship in Yemen—the USS *Cole*—killing seventeen military personnel and causing damage to the ship. It's been said that al-Qaeda viewed this attack as so successful, it spurred them on to plan a further terror campaign to carry out on US soil the following year.

In the aftermath of the terrorist attacks on September 11, 2001, there was much discussion and debate about how the Unites States should respond. Should we go directly after bin Laden? After all, he did take responsibility for the act. Should we take a wait-and-see approach, remaining cautious and watchful but not quick to undertake any sort of military action? Should we try a diplomatic approach or go in all-out militarily right from the start?

Most Americans, it seemed, were all for that last option: We were angry, and we wanted retribution. We wanted more than just a videotape of a man thousands of miles away saying, "Yes, I did it." We wanted him hunted down. We wanted him caught. We wanted him to pay for what he and his people had done to us—a natural response, I think, when something so horrific has been perpetrated against a population.

It didn't take long for our government to decide to go the military route, and we chose Afghanistan as our starting point. The Taliban, the reasoning went, had been harboring bin Laden and al-Qaeda, which meant they were our enemy; as President George W. Bush said at the time, "Either you are with us, or you are with the terrorists." The Taliban most certainly was not with us.

However, we did try diplomacy first; we know better than to just storm a country with our full military force without any warning. We asked Mullah Omar, the leader of the Taliban, to give bin Laden and his main cohorts to us. In true schoolyard bully fashion, he told us to prove bin Laden had been involved in the September 11 attacks—to provide evidence that he had planned it or in any way helped to have it carried out. If we could do that, Omar said, he would turn bin Laden and the others over to a neutral country wherein he could stand trial.

And to that President Bush said, "We know he's guilty. Turn him over." Because the United States does not respond to threats. We do not let other nations—and particularly the likes of the Taliban—think that they can push us around.

When Mullah Omar still would not comply, we had no choice but to enter Afghanistan militarily. This we did in the form of sending special forces and lending air support to the Afghan Northern Alliance, a group led by the heads of several ethnic groups that had been at war with the Taliban since its rise to power. Together, and with the help of our allies, including NATO countries such as the United Kingdom and Australia, we destroyed al-Qaeda training camps and upset the terrorist network's operating structure by killing or capturing many of its operatives; the Northern Alliance succeeded at last in its goal of retaking Kabul, the capital of Afghanistan, from the Taliban.

However, Osama bin Laden continued to elude us. We knew he was there; shortly after we invaded Afghanistan, the US State Department released to the media a video of bin Laden taking responsibility for the September 11 attacks in the United States, saying he and al-Qaeda were the ones who planned it and carried it out. In the video, bin Laden was speaking with a group of associates, and it was verified that this meeting took place in Afghanistan shortly before we removed the Taliban from control of the government.

These admissions of responsibility—I would not call it guilt, because at no time did bin Laden ever appear remorseful for what he and al-Qaeda had done; just the opposite, he rejoiced in it—continued on for several years as we followed his trail around the Middle East, centering mostly on Afghanistan and neighboring Pakistan. Periodically, he would release new tapes that discussed the attacks and the overall fatwa he had issued against the United States. As if we needed further proof, after two years of investigation, our government-appointed 9/11 Commission officially confirmed that bin Laden and al-Qaeda had designed, planned, and orchestrated the attacks.

And so we continued our search. Along the way, though we had not yet found bin Laden, we were able to capture or kill almost two thirds of the highest officials within al-Qaeda. The progress was slow but steady, and we continued to follow all leads that came to us regarding bin Laden's whereabouts. Finally, in 2011, we got the tip we needed and managed to find him in Abbottabad, Pakistan, holed up in a fortress-like compound. Under President Obama's direct order, and under the command of the Joint Special Operations Command, a group of at least twenty Navy SEALs undertook a covert operation to infiltrate the compound. They located bin Laden, and in the midst of a firefight, he was killed. DNA from the body, when compared to samples retained from his deceased sister, confirmed his identity, and he was buried at sea according to Islamic custom.

Since the death of Osama bin Laden, the world has breathed a sigh of relief that the man behind some of the worst acts of terror in history is no longer on this planet. However, his death has not meant that al-Qaeda has ceased to be. Since he had set up the organization to be stateless, with operatives around the world and no set locus of operations, it can and continues to exist anywhere there are people who are interested in the cause and who are willing to undergo the training.

Most recently, al-Qaeda was seen supporting Sunni sympathizers and fighting in opposition to Syrian president Bashar Al-Assad. Their efforts were so effective in this conflict that afterward, the organization saw its ranks increase in size within the country, where before they had been negligible—perhaps due in part to Al-Assad's earlier claim that he believed the al-Qaeda organization did not even exist. This is not an irrational claim; the demographics of al-Qaeda are largely unknown, and its worldwide operations are so loosely linked it's difficult to pin down definite associations between events, splinter groups, and the overall operation. When Osama bin Laden was taken out, documents recovered from his compound did show some numbers but nothing current; they said that in 2002 there were 170 operatives and leaders in the core al-Qaeda organization, but it would seem there had to be many more given the breadth and scope of some of their attacks.

Indeed, four years later it was estimated that there were several thousand al-Qaeda operatives in at least forty countries around the world. Then again, 2009 estimates postulated there were three hundred members at most. Whether this is actual fluctuating membership, a lack of record keeping, or typical al-Qaeda covert operations is difficult to say; no matter the cause, not knowing how many individuals are considered members of al-Qaeda at any given time does help to confound efforts that are raised against them.

One of the great debates tied to this issue is whether or not al-Qaeda would and could exist without Osama bin Laden. This question has arisen particularly surrounding his death, both before and after. When the organization first became known to the world in the aftermath of the September 11 terrorist attacks, it was portrayed as being massive, with countless secret operatives hiding out in "sleeper cells" around the world, all trained, armed, and ready to rise up and be "activated" at a moment's notice. These were people who could blend right into society alongside us; they could be our neighbors, our coworkers, anyone at all, and we would never know it. Whether this was a fact or a rumor spread by al-Qaeda itself, the media, or simply the public's word of mouth, it was a terrifying prospect—that we had already been infiltrated by the enemy and we could not even tell who the enemy was. In this sense, it could be said this was an effective terrorism tactic in that it worked to keep people feeling scared and unprotected by their government, who could be seen as failing to prevent these operatives from entering the country. (Though see chapter eight for more on how the US government and military have reacted to the 9/11 attacks and worked to keep our country safe in their wake.)

The "sleeper cell" theory has to some extent been proven true: The al-Qaeda groups that carried out the embassy bombings in Dar es Salaam and Nairobi followed a sleeper-cell model; though the nineteen hijackers who died while perpetrating the September 11 attacks had already been living in the United States for some time, they were not considered a sleeper cell because they were in the country on a specific mission, not simply awaiting orders and commands to obey. A 2002 Fox News report estimated there may be up to five thousand individuals in the United States who can be linked to Osama bin Laden and/or al-Qaeda.

Our own government officials have positively identified sleeper cells as a target of their war on terror both before and after the terrorist attacks of September 11, 2001. In January of that year, Richard Clarke, former national coordinator for security, infrastructure protection, and counterterrorism for the United States, had officially warned Secretary of State Condoleezza Rice that al-Qaeda definitely had a presence in the United States, likely in the form of sleeper cells. After the 9/11 attacks, fearing additional cells might be activated to carry out further similar attacks, the FBI immediately put finding them at the top of their priorities list.

In December 2001, President George W. Bush asserted that in the nation's war on terror, the government would "discover and destroy sleeper cells" as part of a mission to take down the al-Qaeda terrorist network. In July 2002, Secretary of Defense Donald Rumsfeld testified before the Senate Armed Services Committee that al-Qaeda operated in more than sixty countries, including the United States, and that even if we discover and stop one terrorist plot, there will be dozens more to pop up and take its place—all carried out by sleeper cells. This sentiment was echoed in subsequent years by the likes of Senator Chuck Grassley of Iowa, Attorney General John Ashcroft, and Under Secretary Asa Hutchinson, who claimed that al-Qaeda had sent representatives to California and New York a decade earlier to begin training in urban warfare and raising money for future attacks; some of the 9/11 plane hijackers lived among us for four years prior to their attacks, and various sleeper cells had lived in parts of Africa for five years before the 1998 embassy bombings.

The list of affirmations goes on and on. In the United States, at least, it is a given that al-Qaeda sleeper cells exist, though these days there are far fewer than there used to be (again, see chapter eight for more on the US government and military's response to and war on terrorism). So though it would appear that, worldwide, al-Qaeda itself has been sleeping somewhat in the wake of its most powerful leader and mastermind's demise, this may be just a false front. Al-Qaeda has claimed its acts, such as the September 11 terrorist attacks, as victories, but its war is not yet won. They still have work to do in their ongoing attempts to defeat the West. Fortunately, the United States government and military are, as always, ready and watching.

Eight

In the aftermath of the terrorist attacks of September 11, 2001, it was not unusual to hear people advocate our going to war to right the wrong that had been done to us. Days, even hours afterward, before the smoke cleared at Ground Zero in New York City, people were calling for vengeance, and could anyone blame them? This was a massive atrocity that had happened, leaving us all hurt and in shock and, above all, angry. We wanted to know who had done this to us, and we wanted them to pay.

That time would come. It would take President George W. Bush only nine days to take to the nation's airwaves and promise the people of this great country that he was initiating a war on terror that would begin with seeking out and finding al-Qaeda wherever it may be, but it would not stop there. He told us we had a fight ahead of us against an unclear and elusive enemy, and warned other countries that they could be with us or with the terrorists, but not both. We would pursue any nations that knowingly harbored, financed, or in any way condoned terrorists and terrorist acts. We would utilize diplomacy, of course, and the president urged all Americans to do the same in their daily lives—to not take out their anger and frustrations on people who had nothing to do with the attacks, namely Muslims, who suffered a great and sometimes violent backlash during that period.

At that time, President Bush unveiled his plan to start the now ubiquitous Department of Homeland Security to focus on this war on terror, in which, as he famously said, we would not tire, falter, or fail. And we have not. It might not be front page news right now, but as you have already seen in this book, the US government and military are always on guard, even when it is not immediately obvious.

Let's take a look now at some of the ways in which our government and armed forces work and have worked to keep us all safe.

Our History with Terrorism

Although much of the general public did not become aware of terrorism and al-Qaeda until after September 11, 2001, it is something that has been around and within the United States for a very long time. In our country, it's said to date back even to before the Civil War, when a man named John Brown led armed attacks to abolish slavery, aiming to force the government into a new pattern through creating fear in its citizens. (Brown was later executed for treason.) The Ku Klux Klan, or the KKK, was created in 1865 and was known for its acts of intimidation and violence in the furtherance of its racist, anti-Semitic goals; one of its founders is said to have boasted that the group had 555,000 members, 40,000 of which—much like a sleeper cell—could be mustered within days. With no membership documentation, the Klan was an invisible organization similar to al-Qaeda and has been considered politically powerful in certain areas and states.

In later days, we saw people and events such as:

- The Unabomber, aka Ted Kaczynski, a former math professor who opposed industrialism and modern technology; over twenty years, he sent sixteen mail bombs to people involved with technology in protest, killing three and injuring twenty-three.
- The Oklahoma City bombing in 1995, in which Timothy McVeigh and Terry Nichols killed 168 people with a car bomb in front of a federal building. This was done in protest of the government's handling of a siege in Waco, Texas, two years earlier; McVeigh also believed that his act could start a revolution.
- The 1996 Centennial Olympic Park bombing in Atlanta, Georgia, where Eric Rudolph killed two and injured 111 with pipe bombs and shrapnel. His reasoning: He wished to embarrass the US government for its sanctioning of abortion.

However, these were all what we call *domestic terrorism*, meaning they originated from and were carried out by people who were native to the United States, on US soil. As the twentieth century wore on, we became more and more susceptible to and targeted by terrorists from other countries and in other countries. Individuals and organizations, like Osama bin Laden and al-Qaeda, held a grudge against the Western world and the United States in particular and wished to inspire fear in our citizens and residents in order to disrupt our government's ability to rule and thus, in their thinking, weaken our infrastructure and eventually topple our society.

Why did some nations and individuals not like us? Most of it had to do with our foreign policy and some very, very longstanding cultural battles between different peoples. For example, al-Qaeda carried out the World Trade Center bombing in 1993, it was said, because of our economic and military support of Israel and other "dictator countries." Due to some of our allegiances with other nations, we were actually seen as terrorists ourselves when all we sought to do was help those who needed help, to lend money or aid in whatever form we could for those who were waging their own wars on terrorism.

More and more, particularly since that incident in 1993, it seemed that the extremists of the Muslim world were against us for just these reasons, but let me pause here to repeat: These were and are *extremists* who wish to terrorize and bring damage upon our land and our people. Groups like al-Qaeda, while identifying as Islamic, represent a very small minority of ultraconservative, radical, pro-terror Muslims; they do not speak nor act for all who follow Islam, more than 2.5 million of whom are from or reside in the United States.

More and more too, it seemed, our biggest enemy in the radical Muslim world was al-Qaeda. Though the general public might not have known who they were prior to 9/11, our government did, and we watched them closely. We tracked their movements, and we intercepted their communications. Our CIA conducted paramilitary operations and collected intelligence. As noted in the 9/11 Commission's official report, our "homeland defenders faced outward," meaning we knew there were threats coming in from the outside, and we were preparing ourselves for them. Hence, there were units like the IBU-24 on which I served; hence, our missions to the Middle East and at home supported the ongoing—but as yet unofficial—war on terrorism.

Within the government, individuals worked across agencies, both domestic and foreign, to share information and duties to create and maintain the clearest picture of the threat of terrorism worldwide as possible. No resources were held back, and agencies and the intelligence community—including the CIA, the FBI, the State Department, the military, and any and all parties involved in homeland security, as that agency did not yet exist—were mobilized if and when they were needed.

In addition, we had our no-fly lists for commercial airlines, as set out by the Federal Aviation Commission (FAA); airline crews were trained for possible hijacking scenarios, and we did all we could to alert but not alarm people both in and around the aviation industry to be aware of this potential threat. We didn't want people to live in fear, just to know that the possibility was out there, and the more we all worked together and did our parts, the more protected and prepared we would be when the time came.

Did this mean we expected plane attacks? No, we did not. But that's only because, in all honesty, we didn't expect any one thing; we expected *everything*. As I've mentioned before, during the time I was in the IBU-24, the FBI and other governmental agencies were collecting information and intelligence on any potential threats to areas such as New York City from all angles: by air, yes, but also by water and on land. In trying to keep the people of the United States safe, we left all options open and followed every pathway we could find to uncover any terrorism plots that might exist at present or in the future. Along the way, we found some and some found us, and we were able to stop them or follow them until we were sure that they wouldn't be carried out. Did we have leads on the September 11 attacks? Did we know they were going to happen? This is what many people ask—what people have asked even me, knowing my history in the military and particularly in antiterrorism support.

And my answer always is, "Don't you think that if we had known, we would have done something to stop them?"

US Military and Government Response to the September 11 Attacks

The United States military has been in existence since the founding of our first standing army, known as the Continental Army, on June 14, 1775, to fight in the Revolutionary War. And since then we have always been on guard. No matter the branch—army, navy, air force, marines, reserves, coast guard—it is part of our sworn duty to protect the people and possessions of the United States; everything we do is focused on this one goal. Who better, then, to lead the charge in the war on terrorism that began in September 2001?

Since the 9/11 terrorist attacks on the United States began with airplanes, they are what we will start with as well. Within US aviation there are two agencies that play important roles in keeping our airspace safe: the Federal Aviation Administration (FAA), which is an agency of the US Department of

Transportation and has authority to oversee all civil aviation, and the North American Aerospace Defense Command (NORAD), a joint agency of the United States and Canada, headquartered in Colorado, that provides airspace warnings and defense for the continent. Between these two agencies, there is a procedure that if the FAA becomes aware of an incidence of hijacking, it notifies NORAD and can request that NORAD send out an escort aircraft. This means, for example, that a fighter jet will approach the plane in question, the one that is presumed to be hijacked, and follow it in order to observe anything unusual and report back. The escort plane can also assist with search and rescue.

On the morning of September 11, 2001, the FAA did indeed notify NORAD that four commercial airplanes had been hijacked. Unfortunately, for as quickly as the events unfolded, and possibly because the hijackers of the planes had turned off the planes' transponders or altered their transmissions, making them difficult to track via radar, NORAD's escort planes—two F-15 fighter jets utilizing their afterburners to fly supersonically—were unable to reach the hijacked aircraft before they crashed into the World Trade Center, the Pentagon, and in Pennsylvania. The usual procedure was followed, but as these events were anything but usual, we cannot expect the results to be the same as they would have been in a "normal" hijacking scenario. We saw this happen again and again throughout the ordeal: It wasn't that we weren't prepared. It was that what was happening was beyond anything we'd thought a group of humans were capable of doing.

Perhaps for this reason, most of the military and governmental responses to the 9/11 terrorist attacks took place after the fact. When all was said and done, that was when we were pushed into gear. Mere hours after the attacks ended, as the search and rescue efforts got underway, there were those in the government who were already figuring out how to compensate the victims of this tragedy—to offer financial help to those who had lost family members in the attacks and needed some temporary assistance to keep going. President Bush was meeting with his cabinet members and advisors, forming the tenets of the war on terrorism, which he would announce in an address to the nation on September 20, 2001. The immediate goals of this war were to bring the perpetrators of the attacks, namely Osama bin Laden, to justice, and to root out and destroy al-Qaeda wherever it may have been hiding.

However, there would be a second leg as well. The US war on terrorism, even in those early days, also looked to the future, where it aimed to prevent the formation of new terrorist groups like al-Qaeda. Once we brought them down—and we would indeed bring them down; President Bush assured us of that quite assertively—we didn't have to worry about them anymore, but that did not mean we could let our guards down. On the contrary, though our eyes had been open before September 11, now they were *wide* open, and we would not let anything like this happen again. Not by al-Qaeda, not by any group copying al-Qaeda. As President Bush so famously said, fool me once, shame on you. Fool me twice, shame on me. We would not let ourselves be taken again.

Accomplishing these goals would, of course, require funding, manpower, and cooperation between our military, our government, and other nations as well. Again, President Bush told all those listening—and those not listening, who would surely hear of it anyway; this was a monumental speech delivered at a true turning point in history—that any nation that was with the terrorists was not with the United States, a modern take on the "the enemy of my friend is my enemy" adage. For those countries that did choose to harbor terrorists, there would be economic and military sanctions, meaning we would withhold any financial aid we were giving them at present, any they might need in the future, and any military protection we provided for the duration of their complicity.

On our end, we increased our efforts and capabilities in global surveillance and in coordinating between government agencies, ensuring each and all had the intelligence they needed to get the work done. Though this might not seem like the biggest deal in this entire effort, never underestimate the power of knowledge and information. Without it, we would not have found al-Qaeda to begin with; we would not have eventually found our way to Osama bin Laden. Perhaps, without information, we would not be able to foresee and forestall the next attempted terrorist attack on our homeland.

The next logical step in our war on terrorism was, of course, our invasion of Afghanistan in order to unseat the Taliban governmental regime and root out any al-Qaeda operatives who were being harbored there, including, it was said, Osama bin Laden. This assault, in which we were aided by British military forces as well as the Afghan Northern Alliance on the ground, was the second-largest operation in the war on terror outside of our borders and the largest directly connected to terrorism itself.

At home, our government continued to work tirelessly to protect us against further terrorist attacks. In 2001, Congress passed the USA PATRIOT (United and Strengthening America by Providing Appropriate Tools Required to Intercept and Obstruct Terrorism) Act, which would work to increase security in many areas of the government and the nation by, among other things:

- Establishing and increasing funding for counterterrorist activities.
- Authorizing the military to provide assistance, on the request of the attorney general, when incidents involving weapons of mass destruction arose.
- Expanding the National Electronic Crime Task Force, a team comprised of Secret Service agents, private sector organizations and individuals, and scholars working together to combat criminal activity using electronics such as computers.
- Increasing the government's capabilities of collecting data and information about suspected terrorists through surveillance.
- Preventing money laundering to finance terrorist groups or acts, and prosecuting when it did occur
- Giving greater authorization to the attorney general and to the Immigration and Naturalization Service (INS) in investigating breaches of law and enforcing laws.
- Providing monetary rewards to those who provided information that helped the Department of Justice fight and prevent terrorism.

Additionally, in 2002 Congress passed and President Bush signed the Homeland Security Act, which brought together under one umbrella the disparate fields within the CIA, FBI, and other investigative entities that had already been working on the subject for years.

The FBI

Immediately after the 9/11 terrorist attacks, the FBI launched what became the largest criminal investigation in US history, with the largest crime scenes in FBI history. Known as PENTTBOM (Pentagon/Twin Towers Bombing Investigation), the unprecedented inquiry eventually involved four thousand FBI agents—that was more than half of the entire body of the FBI—and three thousand other personnel, all of them working around the globe and, often, around the clock. There were SWAT team members; FBI rookies; former soldiers, state troopers, and detectives; Special Forces members; and agents specializing in psychology, terrorism, and various languages.

The initial main goal of the independent PENTTBOM commission was to identify the hijackers and those who provided them with the funding and the training to carry out their terrorist missions. Its secondary goal was, like all other facets of the military and government working on the issue at the time, to prevent any potential future attacks. During the course of the PENTTBOM investigation, the FBI followed more than half a million leads and acted upon several hundred thousand tips called and sent in by members of the public at large. Together, they conducted almost 200,000 interviews and reviewed millions of bits of paper from immigration records to parking receipts to interrogation transcripts. They also examined bank and telephone records, which proved to be the most important evidence they had in reconstructing the hijackers' movements prior to the attacks and continued to help them keep track of al-Qaeda's activities for years to come.

The PENTTBOM team also logged more than 150,000 pieces of evidence including debris from the sites of impact in New York; Washington, DC; and Pennsylvania. They created a timeline of the hijackers' activities prior to the attacks that stretched on for eight thousand entries.

Within the PENTTBOM unit, specialized groups were formed to focus on specific areas of the investigation, such as the airline flights, the parts of the plot that traced back to Saudi Arabia (all but one of the hijackers was Saudi Arabian), and anything that involved the use of a computer. One group, named Project Backtrack, looked through millions of records from passenger airlines and found almost two hundred flights the nineteen hijackers had taken in the decade before the attacks, including what appeared to be six practice and surveillance flights between May and August 2001.

PENTTBOM was the effort that cracked the case wide open; within only a few days, the FBI had identified all nineteen men who had hijacked the planes used in the 9/11 attacks—in part because the terrorists had made it easy for them. They all had been living in the United States for some time and had made no efforts to conceal their true identities, not even on the passports and credit cards they were using when traveling or in the names they gave for the airplanes' manifests. Four of their passports survived the crashes in whole or in part; two of them had been doctored in ways that were deemed to be associated with al-Qaeda.

One of the intact passports was found in a suitcase belonging to Mohamed Atta, the "ringleader" of the hijacking operation (who, by the way, had one group within the team dedicated solely to him). The luggage, which had missed a connecting flight and thus was not involved in any of the plane crashes, also contained papers showing the identities of and details of all eighteen of his cohorts, including dates of birth, addresses, and visa statuses.

The next phase of PENTTBOM involved linking these terrorists' names to al-Qaeda, which did not prove to be very difficult as many already had files within the US government's intelligence agencies. Once they identified one man, they were able to trace his connections to the others and so on and so on until the entire team was assembled. From there, they could also identify alleged accomplices in cities across the United States who might have helped the hijackers prepare for their mission in some way. FBI agents also investigated and visited locations where the terrorists had been seen or were known to frequent, such as flight schools where they learned to fly commercial aircraft, neighborhoods in which they lived, and restaurants.

In following the trails of these nineteen men back to al-Qaeda, the FBI and CIA logically could pin the crimes committed on Osama bin Laden; as the group's leader, he would undoubtedly have been the mastermind behind the attacks. The agencies even intercepted communications that indicated as much on September 11, the day on which the attacks took place. As noted earlier, it was believed that bin Laden denied responsibility for the attacks early on but later did own up, admitting full culpability through a series of audio and video interviews and statements. This position was maintained until his death in 2011.

However, the FBI's investigations did not end after identifying the attackers. Almost as important as who had done it was why they had done it: What had motivated these men to murder thousands of people and destroy billions of dollars' worth of property? This question was answered in part in a series of letters recovered after the attacks on September 11—one in Atta's lost suitcase, one in a hijacker's car parked at Washington Dulles International Airport, and one at the site where United flight 93 crashed in Pennsylvania.

Each letter was hand written, four pages long, and identical to all the others; that is, there was one letter copied and given to each hijacker. The letters appeared to serve not just as reminders and directions for what was to be carried out and how the terrorists were to go about it, but as encouragement and assurance that what they were doing was right. They included passages such as:

- "Do not make apparent on you the appearance of confusion and tightness of nerves and be happy smiling with your chest expanding and content because you are doing an act that Allah loves and is content with…Smile in the face of adversity all young men for you are going forth to the everlasting paradise."
- "Then you will see the plane after it stops then it will take off…Then do remembrance of Allah as Allah had mentioned in his book 'Oh Allah, pour upon us patience and make firm our feats and make us victorious upon the people of unbelief.'"

- "Do supplication for yourself and to all your brothers that they will be able to conquer and be victorious in hitting the targets...do not be fearful."
- "When the hour of zero comes, breathe deeply and open your chest welcoming death in the way of Allah...let the last part of your speech be, 'There is No God but Allah and Muhammad is his messenger.' And after it, if God is willing, the meeting in the high paradise."

The letters also gave the hijackers instructions about when to pray and what to pray for, to "train" themselves to listen and obey "100 percent," to prepare their weapons ("Let each one sharpen his razor"), and most of all to remain vigilant but feel at ease with what they were about to do, as it was Allah's will—as they interpreted it, of course.

The PENTTBOM investigation continued for years. Well into 2004, the team was profiled in the *Washington Post*—the first time the operation was discussed publicly. At that time, we learned not only about the vital information the team had uncovered but the smaller details of their work, such as returning victims' recovered items to their families and briefing them as well as Congress, the House-Senate inquiry committee, and the independent 9/11 Commission on any pertinent discoveries they had made. The team even set up a website and a phone number where interested parties could log on or call to receive information about their loved ones.

Also by that time, the team was down to a mere ten members, as the bulk of the work had already been completed. The remaining associates reviewed military and CIA intelligence reports on a daily basis, worked with prosecutors on the case against Zacarias Moussaoui (a French citizen who was later discovered to have been involved in the September 11 terrorist plot, though he did not physically carry it out; he was the only person in the United States charged in connection to them), and kept up with interrogation reports from Guantanamo Bay and other facilities where alleged al-Qaeda operatives were being held at the time.

Since September 11, 2001, the PENTTBOM team has been essential to the process of identifying, finding, apprehending, and prosecuting when possible other suspected al-Qaeda associates and terrorists in training, including the following:

- Mushabib al-Hamlan, an al-Qaeda member who had trained at their camps and personally met Osama bin Laden. Hamlan was thought to have been in line to become one of the September 11 hijackers, even going so far as to obtain a US visa. However, he backed out at the last minute when his mother fell ill. By 2004, he was in custody in Saudi Arabia.
- Mohamed al-Qahtani, a Saudi citizen who had also been in place as a hijacker for the 9/11 attacks. He did not get his chance to participate because when he attempted to enter the United States with a visa in August 2001, it was suspected that he was trying to immigrate—to stay here permanently—so he was turned away. Still, he was apprehended in June 2002 and remains at the Guantanamo Bay detention center in Cuba.
- Ali Saleh Kahlah Marri, a US university graduate PENTTBOM investigated for twenty months after

the September 11 attacks based on a call he had placed to a United Arab Emirates phone number associated with Mustafa al-Hawsawi, an al-Qaeda member who was also the organizer and financier of the 9/11 terrorist attacks. PENTTBOM had Marri arrested as a material witness in late 2001, and he was later affirmatively identified as an al-Qaeda agent. President Bush personally called him a "sleeper agent."
- Adnan El Shukrijumah, a known al-Qaeda operative who has been said to be involved in planning another attack on American soil. Unfortunately, Shukrijumah remains at large.

In the thirteen years since the September 11 terrorist attacks, the FBI has overwhelmingly increased its abilities and capacities to keep the American public as safe as possible and, as a result, has identified and broken up terrorist cells in the United States, dismantled terrorist networks around the globe, and cut off the means, including monetary, of those who support terrorist organizations and missions. This has included the following:

- US citizen Rezwan Ferdaus, who was charged with being part of a plot to fly large, remote-controlled aircrafts loaded with C-4 into the Pentagon and US Capitol building. He was also charged with attempting to provide support to al-Qaeda in order to carry out attacks on US soldiers stationed overseas. (October 2001).

- The charging of Michael Finton, aka Talib Islam, who worked on a plot to blow up a federal building in Springfield, Illinois, with a truck bomb; he was sentenced to twenty-eight years in prison. (May 2011).
- The arrests of two men for planning to attack a military processing center in Seattle with grenades and machine guns. (June 2011).
- The arrest of Khalid Ali-M Aldawsari, a Saudi citizen residing in Texas, for purchasing chemicals and equipment used in making improvised explosive devices (IEDs). One of his supposed targets was the home of former president George W. Bush. Aldawsari was also arrested for attempted use of a weapon of mass destruction. (February 2011).
- Charging five members of al-Qaeda for a plot to attack United States and UK targets, including using suicide bombers in New York City's subway system in 2009. (July 2010).
- A life sentence for Faisal Shahzad, a US citizen born in Pakistan, who drove a car bomb into Times Square in New York City. (June 2010).
- Charges against Umar Farouk Abdulmutallab, a Nigerian national who attempted to bomb a Northwest Airlines flight on Christmas Day in 2009. (January 2010).
- Charging and convicting Oussama Abdullah Kassir, a Swedish citizen, for participating in the attempted establishment of a jihad training camp in Oregon and for running terrorist websites. (May 2009).
- Convictions of three men, known as the Toledo

Terror Cell, who conspired to recruit and train terrorists in the United States to attack, among others, US military personnel in Iraq, and for providing material support to terrorists. (June 2008).
- Charges and a forty-seven-year prison sentence for Hemant Lakhani, who was trying to sell shoulder-fired missiles to a terrorist group (which was really an FBI group creating a sting) that would use the missiles to down commercial aircrafts. (April 2005).

And these are only a few of many, many times the FBI has stopped terror-related activities, both attempted and planned, in the last decade-plus.

Spurred on by their increased success rate in identifying and stopping terrorist plots, the FBI has also increased its focus on general high-level crimes that have plagued the public in this country. Working with local and state law enforcement teams, the FBI has increased its investigations into white collar crimes, corruption, and computer- and Internet-related crimes. Its advanced experience in evidence collection and victim identification, as had been put into practice after the September 11 terrorist attacks, have allowed them to work with recovery efforts following natural disasters and other crises. These have included the following:

- A five-year investigation into the collapse of Enron, a major US energy company that committed accounting fraud by using loopholes to hide billions of dollars' worth of failed projects. Then the company went bankrupt, leaving its employees and

stockholders with nothing. The investigation, initiated in December 2001, was one of the largest and most-complex in FBI history.
- Operation Joint Hammer, in which the FBI joined an ongoing, worldwide effort to uncover child pornography rings. More than sixty people in the United States were arrested for trading child pornography. (December 2008).
- The arrest of fifty-seven suspected members of the Mafia in New York. The leaders of the Gambino organized crime family were indicted. (February 2008).
- Operation Joker's Wild, which led to federal convictions of ten members of the F13 street gang. In total, 102 individuals were included in four indictments. (January 2009).
- The apprehension of some of the FBI's Ten Most Wanted Fugitives: Clayton Lee Waagner, a convicted bank robber and antiabortion activist (December 2001); Warren Steed Jeffs, leader of a polygamous sect (August 2006); Jon Savarino Schillaci (June 2008); Michael Registe (August 2008); Emigdio Preciado, Jr., who attacked police officers in 2000 (July 2009); and Edward Eugene Harper (July 2009).

Military Response to September 11, 2001

Since the 9/11 terrorist attacks, our armed forces have been steadily increasing not only in size but in focus and determination to win the war on terrorism. Directly after the attacks, the

US military saw a surge in enlistments as young people from all walks of life signed up to do their parts in finding justice for our nation. Many who had been directly affected by the attacks or their aftermath joined the military afterward as a commitment to the American people and to assist in finding the culprits, apprehending them, and ensuring they were given the punishment they deserved. Many who had not been involved but could only watch the attacks from afar enlisted as a means of showing their support for our country in such a difficult time.

It took only three days after the attacks for the US Congress to pass a resolution called the "Authorization for Use of Military Force (AUMF)," Pub. L. 107-40. This gave our government the ability to utilize our armed forces with "necessary and appropriate force" against anyone found to be responsible for the 9/11 attacks or anyone who assisted, supported, or harbored those who carried out the plot. After Congress passed the resolution, President George W. Bush signed it into practice on September 18, 2001.

In part, the AUMF act reads:

> Whereas, on September 11, 2001, acts of treacherous violence were committed against the United States and its citizens; and
>
> Whereas, such acts render it both necessary and appropriate that the United States exercise its rights to self-defense and to protect United States citizens both at home and abroad; and
>
> Whereas, in light of the threat to the national security and foreign policy of the United States posed by these grave acts of violence; and

Whereas, such acts continue to pose an unusual and extraordinary threat to the national security and foreign policy of the United States; and

Whereas, the President has authority under the Constitution to take action to deter and prevent acts of international terrorism against the United States...

[T]he President is authorized to use all necessary and appropriate force against those nations, organizations, or persons he determines planned, authorized, committed, or aided the terrorist attacks that occurred on September 11, 2001, or harbored such organizations or persons, in order to prevent any future acts of international terrorism against the United States by such nations, organizations, or persons.

Although the name al-Qaeda does not appear anywhere in the text of the act, it is often cited as justification—and rightfully so—to pursue the terrorist network around the world through continued US military actions. This is the act that allowed us the ability to enter Afghanistan in search of Osama bin Laden less than one month after the terrorist attacks in our country, which President George W. Bush called at the time not just an act of terrorism but "acts of war." Even in this light, we first attempted to resolve our issues with Afghanistan—namely, that the country was harboring bin Laden and al-Qaeda, allowing them to host their terrorist training grounds on Afghan soil—through diplomacy. We gave the Taliban an ultimatum: Hand over all individuals known to be associated with al-Qaeda, tell us everything you know about bin Laden, and ban all terrorists from Afghanistan or get ready to pay the consequences. The Taliban's leadership did not immediately say no to all these demands but needed, they said, to assemble a religious council to debate and decide upon a course of action. Two days later, Bush upped the ante by demanding that the Taliban hand over bin Laden himself and not just banish terrorists but demolish all al-Qaeda bases within Afghanistan.

To the surprise of many, the Taliban's religious council swiftly issued a fatwa (a legal opinion or decree handed down by an Islamic religious leader, of which there were one thousand on the council) against Osama bin Laden, telling him to leave the country. They also expressed dismay over what had happened in the United States on September 11 and called on the United Nations to conduct an independent investigation of the attacks. The council, however, was not so compassionate on all counts. Speaking directly to President Bush, they said that if he invaded Afghanistan, all Muslims would be called upon to join the jihad.

The United States government and military—and, indeed, its people—have never taken well to threats, and this occasion was no exception. Just as quickly as the Taliban's religious council had formed and shared its opinions, so did we: As White House spokesperson Ari Fleischer said, the time for talk had ended; it was now time for us to take action. The Taliban, of course, did not like this response and basically said that they were ready to take us on and would ultimately defeat us.

It went back and forth like this for some time. The Taliban demanded proof that Osama bin Laden had orchestrated the September 11 attacks; we provided it. Mullah Omar, the leader of the Taliban, refused to accept it. Finally, he agreed to send bin Laden to Pakistan, where he could be tried by an international tribunal, but the Pakistani president vetoed it, saying he could not guarantee bin Laden's safety there.

The Taliban then demanded more evidence of bin Laden's guilt and said if they got it, they would try him themselves in an Afghan court. By this point, we knew we could not trust them on this, and we denied the request, reiterating our demands that they hand over all al-Qaeda leaders or risk inciting the destruction of their ruling party.

On October 7, 2001, US military forces entered Afghanistan to take down the Taliban regime.

We started with air strikes in Kabul, Kandahar, and Jalalabad, targeting Taliban military sites and terrorist training camps. Most were damaged or destroyed in days. In the next stage, we targeted Taliban vehicles and cluster bombed Taliban defense sites. We also hit the Tora Bora Mountains east of Kabul, where, it was believed, Taliban and al-Qaeda operatives were hiding in underground bunkers.

As we entered November, the Taliban's front lines had been destroyed, and with the support of much of the world behind us—we already had British, Canadian, and Australian forces working with us in Afghanistan, and now Germany, France, Italy, Japan, and others offered their assistance as well—our ground troops advanced on Kabul. This included the CIA's Special Activities Division, the Army Special Forces, and other units from the US Special Operations command as well as Afghanistan's Northern Alliance.

On November 9, the city of Mazari-I Sharif fell after a short but bloody battle between the Taliban and the Northern

Alliance soldiers as well as our Special Forces Operational Detachment A-595, CIA paramilitary officers, our Air Force Combat Control Team, and, of course, our air support. When the Alliance captured the city's main military base and airport, the Taliban retreated. Losing this city was a major hit to the group and one we had not expected to come so quickly. We now had a central base from which to operate and an airport to send out planes for reconnaissance and humanitarian aid. (The six million people in Afghanistan under Taliban rule were living in poverty and starving; part of our goal in this infiltration was to alleviate that as best we could.)

Three days later, the Taliban left Kabul as well, and within one more day all provinces along the Afghanistan-Iran border became free as well. When the remaining Taliban stronghold in the north fell, they were forced to retreat to the south, where they bunked up in caves with al-Qaeda forces in Tora Bora. Again, we bombed the mountains, and our CIA and Special Forces agents worked with local warlords to plan further attacks on the groups.

By the end of the month, the only place the Taliban remained was in Kandahar, and through another brutal battle, Mullah Omar commanded his people to remain defiant—until he quietly slipped out of the city on December 7 and retreated into the mountains. At that point, it seemed, the Taliban's leaders gave up, most of them fleeing to Pakistan. Then the last border town surrendered, and finally Afghanistan was no longer under Taliban control.

However, that did not mean that the fighting ended. We still had al-Qaeda and bin Laden to think about. Its operatives continued to battle on at Tora Bora against a league of tribal

Afghan fighters backed on land and in the air by the US Delta Force and UK Special Forces. At one point, al-Qaeda did agree to a truce and to surrender its weapons, but it soon became clear that this was a ploy to allow bin Laden to escape into neighboring Pakistan. After that, the fighting resumed, but by December 17 we had overtaken every cave complex. Unfortunately, no leaders of the al-Qaeda organization could be found.

A Never-Ending Battle

As was said so often at the time, we had al-Qaeda on the run. Their flight clearly showed their guilt and their fear of being caught, of answering for the terrible things they had done. For us, it meant that our battle was nowhere near over yet. As President Bush had vowed while speaking to the American people, we would not yield, would not rest, and would not relent in waging the battle for freedom and security.

In the wake of the Taliban's loss of power in Afghanistan, our coalition forces consolidated their position at an airbase just north of Kabul, with outposts in eastern areas to continue the hunt for Taliban and al-Qaeda operatives. At the same time, we assisted the nation with setting up an interim government, led by Hamid Karzai, to try to regain some order and begin rebuilding what the war had destroyed.

These were all good things. But underneath, all the bad things continued to simmer. Al-Qaeda and Taliban fugitives began regrouping in teams of 1,000 to 1,500 men to wage guerilla attacks and possibly a major offensive against the United States and coalition forces. To rout these operatives and try to stave off the attacks, we launched Operation Anaconda, in which Afghan forces waged war in the mountains with the two groups, using the caves for cover from enemy fire. Other missions in 2002 and 2003, conducted with the help of the Australian Special Air Service Regiment, the Canadian Joint Task Force 2, the German KSK, the New Zealand Special Air Service, and the Norwegian Marinejegerkommandoen, worked toward the same purpose.

And to some extent, they worked. They slowed down the Taliban and al-Qaeda insurgent groups. However, just like cockroaches, they would scurry back to their hiding spots but always seemed to come back. It didn't help that there were tribes in Pakistan who were willing to harbor them, and in those sanctuaries the al-Qaeda fighters especially were able to regroup into their guerilla units and conduct raids across the border.

The Taliban, meanwhile, hid out and bided its time in the caves and tunnels of Afghanistan as well as in Pakistan. And in those dark places, they formed their newest devious plans. They also established and ran small, mobile training camps for their militants, and in 2003 they were able to launch an insurgency against the coalition forces. The Taliban would send groups of fifty men at a time to attack our most isolated outposts and hit our bases with IEDs and rockets. One group after another came and went, came and went, in a seemingly never-ending stream of firepower while in the background the Taliban continued building up its forces. At the same time, al-Qaeda was running ambushes on American forces.

By late August 2005, we had had enough. The Taliban had to be put down. In order to accomplish this, we put our troops and our aerial bombardment support behind the Afghan government forces, who advanced upon the Taliban's known positions. The battle lasted for a week, and there were casualties on both sides, but in the end we won this one. The Taliban insurgents were forced out of their holes and sent scrambling, looking for new places to hide.

The year 2006 saw a more positive upswing in Afghanistan. The focus was on rebuilding the nation and its government, with US, British, Australian, Canadian, and Dutch troops all there for support. We were still subjected to battles with the Taliban, some of them exceedingly violent. But we took it all in stride, used our tactical and weapon superiority, and were able to come out on top.

Over the next two years, we were able to renew our goals in Afghanistan as well as our commitment to its people to provide a nation in which they could live free from oppression. Toward this end, in 2008, President Bush sent in close to thirty thousand additional troops; Great Britain sent additional forces in as well. NATO also sent in regular convoys of supplies for both the fighting forces and the Afghan people. And all along we continued to repel the Taliban and al-Qaeda insurgencies that popped up from time to time, attempting to overtake us—though it never worked.

And we kept up our hunt for Osama bin Laden, who was proving to be a difficult man to find. Apparently, the hiding-in-plain-sight tactics he promoted for al-Qaeda's sleeper-cell terrorists around the world worked well for him too because he seemed to be everywhere and nowhere at once. He had been spotted; he had released another video or audiotape. But when we arrived at the place where he had been seen or where we thought his missive had been recorded, he was nowhere to be found. It was like chasing a phantom except that we knew that he was very, very real.

Perhaps the Taliban got tired of bin Laden's disappearing act as well, because by the end of the year word had it that the Taliban had severed any remaining connections it had with al-Qaeda. And the latter, for its part, seemed to be disintegrating as well. Al-Qaeda had fewer than one hundred operatives left in Afghanistan in 2008, and with that number it seemed as though perhaps our goal in that sense had been met. How much damage, after all, could just one hundred people do when they couldn't even come out of hiding?

However, there is always a way; if we have learned nothing else from the 9/11 terrorist attacks, that has been the major lesson. There are also always new goals to aim for, new threats to address, and new enemies to battle—far more of each than I could ever cover in the short space of this book. The war on terrorism has not been a one-time thing; it's not a fight with a clear-cut beginning and an end that we can point to and say, "Well, I'm glad that's over." It is a process. It is a learning experience. And it is a never-ending fight for the lives of the American people and, indeed, people all around the world.

As long as religious and cultural extremists and terrorists continue to hate our way of life and to value violence more than peace, we will have, as they say, our job cut out for us. We—and by this I mean the leaders of our government; our army, navy, air force, marines, reserves, and coast guard; our FBI; our CIA; our embassies; our local and state law enforcement teams; and even our citizens and residents themselves—must remain ever vigilant, always looking up in hope but keeping our feet planted firmly on the ground. We must look toward the future with the sense of optimism the forefathers of this nation handed down to us, with the surety that better days will come and the perseverance to make it so.

Still, of course, we must never forget where we have been. The terrorist attacks of September 11, 2001, changed our lives and our way of life forever; they forced us to rethink and restructure our security measures in public places, our standards and systems for commercial aviation, and our methods of screening immigration applicants, to name just a very few.

And in our personal lives, the 9/11 attacks have shaped the way we think about the world and our nation, and even about ourselves and each other—sometimes in good ways, sometimes in bad ways, though hopefully more of the former than the latter. It is understandable that an event of such enormity and magnitude would engender a whole range of emotions from the public, not the least of which would be anger, frustration, and hatred.

But we cannot allow these feelings to control our lives. We cannot live in fear because of what a small group of people has done to us. To do so would be to say they have won, that they succeeded in terrorizing us, in making us distrustful of our government and its ability to protect us from the worst kind of danger. Yes, it did not fully protect us from what happened on September 11, 2001, but how could they protect us from something that no one saw coming?

As I have said over and over in the pages of this book, although people like to say that America was not paying attention or that our government was sleeping on the job, and that was why the terrorist attacks of September 11, 2001, were allowed to happen, it simply isn't true. We were paying attention; we have always been paying attention. For as long as terrorism has existed, we have known about it. We've known there are people out there who harbor intense dislike for the United States and its people and are willing to go very far to show it. We have even known there is an al-Qaeda and that they've had a very anti-Western agenda to further—and that they focus on us. We've known there have been possibilities of attacks, of truck bombs, of IEDs, of suitcase or backpack nuclear weapons. We have even believed that some terrorist groups could launch missiles at New York City or Washington, DC, or other major cities if they wanted to do so.

But airplanes? Commercial jumbo jets full of passengers and luggage? Flying into highly populated and symbolic buildings? No. That had never seemed likely. It was so far fetched, so outlandish, as to be outside the realm of possibility. Did we ever think of it? I'm sure it came up in a brainstorming meeting at some point, when people were throwing around ideas about what they should be watching for. And watch we have done: There has long been an international no-fly list that bans certain individuals from flying into or within our country. There have long been security checkpoints in airports that scan luggage and passengers for weapons and other contraband, and there has long been limited access in airports for anyone without a ticket. There are immigration procedures to follow when one enters the country and then more hurdles to jump if one wishes to stay for any extended period of time. There are databases of names of people who can't be trusted, files to which all agencies of the government have access as needed. We have long had intelligence, piles and piles of it that grow higher every year.

So how did we miss it then? How did those nineteen

hijackers get onto those four planes and crash them into the World Trade Center, the Pentagon, and—potentially, if the passengers hadn't foiled the plot—the Capitol building or the White House? There are hundreds of reasons I could cite here. Perhaps their names were not on our existing watch lists; it was, after all, as I have already discussed, difficult to pin down the exact enrollment in al-Qaeda. It didn't even keep its own rosters, so how could we be expected to know every single person who identified as one of its adherents?

What's more, the hijackers had come into the United States on legitimate visas for what seemed like legitimate purposes. As far as immigration went, everything they did was legal and above board. Maybe we didn't catch them for this very reason: They were not doing anything that was highly suspicious. They lived among us, they took airline flights across the country, and they enrolled in flight schools for flying lessons. They worked. They ate at restaurants, and they shopped at Walmart. Nothing out of the ordinary there. These are all things any other average American might do in his or her lifetime, which brings up perhaps the most salient revelation of them all: These terrorists acted just like us. And in creating such a perfect imitation, they were able to move among us undetected. We simply accepted them as our next-door neighbors, our coworkers, and the regular guys we passed on the street.

And this is how al-Qaeda managed to catch us by surprise: not because we weren't paying attention, but because they had come up with a method of destruction that was so devious it was nearly undetectable. The hijackers' modus operandi included blending in and acting like regular people—acting like us. (If this is a truly terrifying thought, it should be;

that such monsters could roam among us undetected is gut wrenching and mind bending.) It also included buying regular business-class plane tickets, checking regular luggage, and wearing regular clothing for the flights. In a larger sense, that they used commercial flights was the biggest disguise of all in that the anonymity of it helped them mask themselves. Though they gave their real names and did not alter their appearances in any way, the fact that they appeared to be just another few travelers en route to their destinations that day sadly worked in their favor.

But that does not mean that it will work again. If September 11, 2001, can be considered a miss for our government, a case in which they should have seen it coming and didn't (though of course, as you have read, I wholeheartedly disagree with that), then rest assured that it has been a lesson learned. Either way, whether we should have known about it or not, the 9/11 attacks have forced those of us in the government and military spheres to examine everything we do and ask ourselves: Is this for the good of the American people? Will this keep them safe? Will it prevent anything like September 11 from ever happening again?

Even though I am retired from the navy now, I still ponder such questions as well as where the future might take our country. At times, it can be easy to fall into negativity on the subject; there are so many terrible things going on in the world—famine and disease; abuse of power and of innocent people; religious intolerance; racism, homophobia, and other bigotry; and, it seems sometimes, just death and destruction in all corners—that it's difficult to see the light at the end of the tunnel. When bad things seem to happen over and over again, particularly incidents on the level of the September 11 terrorist attacks, everything can become shrouded in darkness.

But that, I assure you, is not how the world is. The light is always out there, even if it's just a small beacon to remind you that there is a way home. If you ever can't see it, try to remember that there are people out there who are looking out for you 24 hours per day, 7 days per week, and 365 days per year. Those are the people in your military and your government, the ones you have appointed to lead you and the ones who have volunteered to serve for you. You may not always see us; our missions are not always as obvious as navigating a large boat down the waters of the Hudson River off Manhattan, patrolling to keep the city safe. Sometimes we work undercover or in covert operations that you will never hear about, seeking out and apprehending or otherwise dealing with people you will never even know existed. Sometimes we work in offices, staring at computers all day to keep the area known as cyberspace safe for all who utilize it for work and for fun on a daily basis, and to take down those who would use it to plot or carry out their evil deeds. We are on teams like PENTTBOM, the Special Forces, or IBU-24, or we work deep within the FAA or NORAD—organizations you might not think you need in your life, but they are working behind the scenes at all times to keep your *way of life* just as it is.

But then we have our more visible moments, too. We show up when and where we are needed, to assist and organize in times of crisis: when there are earthquakes, hurricanes, or rioting. Our president goes on national TV to talk to us one on one, it seems, about the most pressing issues facing us as Americans every day and how he, as a fellow American, is going to help us through it. Our senators lobby for our rights, and our congressional representatives draft laws that will protect those rights from being violated—as well as laws to punish those who take our rights away. Our courts help us with this too, right up to the Supreme Court.

We even go to other nations and put ourselves literally in the line of fire to protect what we have here at home—who we are, how we live, and even the things we possess. Though some people cannot always see the correlation between their freedom and what the men and women of our military are doing in, for example, Afghanistan or Iraq, there is a direct connection there: Without our military presences in certain countries, they can become havens for terrorists who would plot against us, who would seek to kill us whether at home or abroad. In fighting them on foreign soil, we prevent them from coming here and doing to us as they please. We are preparing; we are preventing.

Most of all, we never sleep, and we are always on watch.

www.ingramcontent.com/pod-product-compliance
Lightning Source LLC
Chambersburg PA
CBHW072045290426
44110CB00014B/1573